SEX SEEN

Sex Seen

THE EMERGENCE OF
MODERN SEXUALITY
IN AMERICA

■

Sharon R. Ullman

UNIVERSITY OF CALIFORNIA PRESS
BERKELEY   LOS ANGELES   LONDON

University of California Press
Berkeley and Los Angeles, California

University of California Press, Ltd.
London, England

© 1997 by
The Regents of the University of California

Library of Congress Cataloging-in-Publication Data

Ullman, Sharon R., 1955–.
    Sex seen: the emergence of modern sexuality in America /
Sharon R. Ullman.
        p.   cm.
    Includes bibliographic references and index.
    ISBN 0-520-20954-0 (cloth: alk. paper).—
ISBN 0-520-20955-9 (pbk.: alk. paper)
        1. Sex customs—United States—History—20th century.
2. Sexual ethics—United States—History—20th century.
I. Title.   HQ18.U5U44   1997
    306.790973—dc 21   97–26151

Printed in the United States of America
9 8 7 6 5 4 3 2 1

The paper used in this publication meets the minimum
requirements of American National Standards for Information
Sciences—Permanence of Paper for Printed Library Materials,
ANSI Z39.48–1984.

To My Mother

Contents

Acknowledgments

Producing this book has taken a long time, and many people have participated over the years. Acknowledgments are a singular pleasure because they provide one with the opportunity to say permanently in print what one might have been too shy to say in person at the moment it counted.

My great gratitude goes to Mary Ryan, who directed this project as a dissertation at the University of California at Berkeley. Leon Litwack and Barbara Christian formed the rest of my exceptional committee. I have never forgotten that this was the academic equivalent of winning the lottery. This work is infinitely better by virtue of Mary's comments, conversation, and unstinting support over many years. That we shared an abiding affection for the Oakland Athletics and, most particularly, for Joe Montana and the San Francisco 49ers made it possible to bridge all controversies and achieve a profound intellectual communion.

I have had generous assistance during many phases of this book. Estelle Freedman was very supportive and encouraging early in the process. The members of the San Francisco Bay Area Gay and Lesbian History Project offered my work and me a safe haven in the 1980s. Eva Peters Hunting and Miriam Schwarzschild opened their homes in Sacramento and New York, respectively, and made my research possible. Friends who offered ideas and meals from the beginning include Carolyn Dean, Nina Silber, Jeff Lena, Louis Hutchins, Matt Dennis, Tom Holt, and Eric Garber. Their help has been immeasurable; their good humor constant.

I must thank the staff at the Sacramento Archive and Museum Collection. During my research, director James Henley, archivist Charlene Gilbert, and most particularly curator Patty Gregory gave me enormous assistance as I waded through hundreds of court cases and county documents. At the Paper Print Collection in the Library of Congress Motion Picture Reading Room, Kathy Loughney was very helpful and patient with numerous last-minute requests. Librarians at the Billy Rose Collection of the New York Public Library, Lincoln Center Branch, provided fine support as well.

Many friends and colleagues have looked at and commented upon portions of this final text. I thank Allan Berubè, Raji Mohan, Jennifer Terry, and Patricia White for their important help at pivotal moments. I am deeply indebted to Jane Caplan, Laurie Bernstein, Bob Weinberg, Amy Green, Joseba Gabilondo, Christia Mercer, Steven Grover, Lisa Henderson, Judy Hiserman, Arl Nadel, Annette Ranck, Kathleen Schardt, Bill Walker, and especially Bob Moeller for sustaining friendships that kept my head and heart going in often difficult times. I want to single out and particularly thank Hannah Schwarzschild for the ways—too many to count—that she helped over the years.

This book could not have been completed without the gracious support of Bryn Mawr College, which funded the leave that made completion possible. Anna Canavan offered invaluable technical assistance. Naomi Schneider, my editor at the University of California Press, has been my biggest (and most patient) booster for many years.

Pieter Judson was one of two people who read and commented on every word that appears here. It was a remarkably generous gesture, and I only wish I could pin any mistakes on him, but that hardly seems fair. Instead he has my eternal gratitude—which should be burden enough.

Stephen Aron also read the entire manuscript, and I want to give him a special acknowledgment. From the first days of graduate school, when he dragged us all off to the track (where he won, I think—I know I didn't), to the recent call advising me that he had "pondered for days" (at my request) titles for this book, Steve has been the intellectual and emotional heart for an extended (and ever-growing) family of scholars and friends. An exceptional historian, he is also a model for how to make the academy a rigorous but truly genial and supportive working community. I cannot thank him enough for his counsel over the years.

My brother, his family, and my father have all been patient supporters and witnesses to this long journey. But my deepest debt is to my mother, Lilian Ullman. My mother always told me there were no limits in life and that I could achieve whatever goal I set. Her death in 1981 spurred me finally to go after one I truly wanted. Having arrived, I thank her yet again.

Chapter One

Pulling off the Bedclothes

He said: "Hello Charlie. Jesus Christ. You ought to have been with me last night. I went to Lafferty's stable and got me a buggy and took a ride out a ways and met a young cunt, and I took her over the levee and fucked her three times, and made her suck my cock."[1]

Charles Harlan told this story to his friend Charlie Stanfield in 1899. A twenty-four-year-old farmhand with a wife and two small daughters, Harlan lived in Sacramento, California—a town of roughly 29,000 people in 1900—during an era often characterized historically by a proscriptive literature emphasizing female purity and male restraint. That one individual's language of desire should differ from that of the literature is hardly surprising. Unfortunately, the existing literature contains little information about the sensibilities of people such as Charles Harlan. How are we to decipher the development and evolution of sexual codes in American history without a sense not only of Charles Harlan's sexual world but of the sexual culture that surrounded him?

Charles Harlan's story is but one of many tales that illustrate the birth pangs of an emerging public vision of sexuality. In the following pages I will look closely at images and language drawn from early-twentieth-century popular culture and from community struggles in order to tell these tales. They will feel uneasily familiar, for they offer an exceptional window onto a sexual past that is nothing less than the beginning of our sexual present.

I

Not surprisingly, most of these stories about sexuality originated in the private realm and came into public view only in strange, even

1

perverse ways. Charles Harlan's narrative was told in a Sacramento criminal court during his trial for rape. Similar tales of sexual woe—often harrowing narratives of abuse—came to light in divorce records and vice investigations. In addition to these chronicles from the legal system, many commentaries were left by middle-class arbiters of public and private behavior, who attempted to police sexuality through moral authority. Their opinions and ideology permeate the documentary evidence.

Yet can we really gain an accurate vision of turn-of-the-century sexual values from the thundering Progressive voices who so dominate the era's records? The archives available to historians are deeply troubled repositories of knowledge. The nature of the archive is obviously a problem in all historical inquiry, but in this case it is a particularly disruptive difficulty because the topic forces an artificial collapse of boundaries between the public and private. Studying everyday sexual culture requires that it be seen, yet sexual practice itself—from which such a visible culture must emanate—takes place almost entirely behind closed doors. Researchers must therefore demand from their data a story that it almost inevitably cannot tell in full.

Yet we can ill afford to abandon the inquiry in disgruntled despair. Sexuality is not only an interesting, if previously undiscussed, element in history but also a driving factor in the twentieth-century United States. How can we make sense of modern American society without taking sexuality into account? How shall we explain our literature, film, television, advertising, or commodity culture—virtually every element of what might be deemed our public culture—as long as sexuality remains historically marginalized? As the twentieth century ends and America plunges into the "culture wars," with vast disagreement over such issues as abortion, homosexuality, AIDS, single motherhood, and the proper construction and containment of the reproductive family—how can we conceptualize what has happened here without focusing on the history of sexuality?

So we are caught between a subject that we have an absolute historical obligation to excavate and an archive that leaves us flabbergasted with its inadequacy and highly compartmentalized nature. Do we need another history of prostitution? We can write as many as we like—for these the records exist—and essential elements of sexual regulation by the state can be explored through traditional archival research. But such surveys cannot really illuminate the questions that so dog us at the end of the century. Where did our public sexual culture come from? How did particular kinds of sexual imagery come to saturate a society that is one of the most prudish in the world? As we attempt to flesh out that set of questions, it is impossible to hang back and wait for the archives to reveal the necessary data; we will have to find it elsewhere.

This book responds to the challenge by posing an alternative approach. In the following chapters I examine a set of interpretative moments and closely read selected material from a variety of archival sites to present the fascinating and complex images of sexuality available to Americans in the early twentieth century. Focusing on small communities and new national popular media, this analysis juxtaposes the language of court records from sex-crime trials and divorce proceedings with the sexual tales told by early film and vaudeville. These widely divergent sources yield startling evidence of a contested sexual culture under vigorous public construction. They reveal the foundations of the sexual system that we take for granted today.

The notion of "modern sexuality" encompasses many possibilities and many judgments. Historians date what is called the "modernization of sexuality" from the period covered in this book. The term refers to the twentieth-century redefinition of sexuality as a means of self-realization rooted in pleasure and unconnected to reproduction. A new value system revolving around desire and sexual fulfillment became prominent; sexual discourse emphatically entered the public realm, and the entire framework for sexual understanding came loose from religious and proscriptive moorings. This dramatic revisioning made sexuality central to personal identity and even to the definition of a successful life.

In attempting to trace the roots of modern sexuality and the processes by which it emerged, this book focuses on a few particularly illustrative ideologies. We live in a society that celebrates female sexuality, is endlessly discomfited by unorthodox sexual practices, insists that pleasurable sex is the key to a good marriage, and believes that sex "sells" just about anything. All of these attitudes were held, though not settled or agreed upon, in the early twentieth century.

This book tracks these ideas at the dawn of the century, demonstrating how they emerged and were ferociously contested.

Many historians have looked to the late nineteenth and early twentieth century to uncover sexual secrets. This is due in no small measure to the elaborate network of social reformers who flourished in this period and who kept very good notes. These people are generally (and often wrongly) grouped under the broad rubric of "Progressives." However, the nature of their reform activities and agendas varied greatly, and their efforts hardly constituted a cohesive movement. Yet those hoping to eradicate moral turpitude did have many ideas in common. Driven by the extraordinary changes caused by large-scale immigration, urbanization, and industrialization, reformers sought out despair and degradation wherever they could find it. Sexual activity proved a productive starting point. The reformers investigated prostitution, white slavery, illegitimacy, seduction, "moral imbecility" (a willingness by a single female to engage in heterosexual sex without remorse), homosexuality, immoral public entertainment, and numerous other signs of "contemptible" sexual behavior. These activists found all manner of such horrors and left a wealth of evidence about certain "deviant" sexual practices from the turn of the century.

The records also tell us much about the reformers' own points of view and biases. Encouraged by an emerging middle-class ethos of particular family values—an ethos relatively new to the nineteenth century—reformers sought to impose a vision that punitively confined sexual activity to marriage and offered an exceedingly narrow interpretation of sexual pleasure. This nineteenth-century sexual "revolution," which the reformers attempted to bring into the twentieth century, overturned (with varying degrees of success) previously long-standing American sexual traditions, such as tacit acceptance of premarital intercourse as long as marriage followed and a recognition of female sexual desire.

This shift in mores is often referred to as the triumph of a "Victorian" sensibility—as amorphous a designation as one can get in the American context. It is more helpful to regard this development as a by-product of the growth of the middle class in a newly industrializing country. This emerging class needed to create a specific moral authority to accompany its expanding political and economic influence. Reform impulses based in the evangelical Christianity of the 1830s and 1840s dealt with prostitution and illegitimacy. By the 1870s and 1880s, a broader coalition of idealists put sexuality and the nuclear family (made more stable by nineteenth-century prosperity and medical advances) at the forefront of social activism. Middle-class women in particular, acting out of genuine concern over the perceived social ills of the late nineteenth century, fanned out across the urban landscape and attempted to take corrective measures.

They saw rampant sexuality as a prime cause of societal decay. Reformers believed that young city dwellers, loosened from the restraints of the father and the family farm, faced the twin devils of industrial poverty and sexual temptation. Never mind that the patriarchal authority of the countryside had long since eroded (as evidenced by earlier reform efforts assaulting the sexual codes of rural America). Reform activists seem not to have considered the possibility that rural migrants might bring their own moral values with them rather than simply being victimized by urban vice. By contrast, foreign immigrants—particularly men—were seen as infectious agents who introduced moral disease from abroad. Foreign women found themselves cast as both victims and purveyors of licentious desire. The "white slavery" prostitution crisis that so alarmed late-nineteenth- and early-twentieth-century reformers was blamed on the immigrant population. Indeed, those concerned by the apparent collapse of American morals and sexual health in the early twentieth century seem to have believed that much of the problem could be traced to bad immigration policies.

As Michel Foucault has pointed out, "silencing"—such as that claimed by these so-called Victorians—is the opposite of quiet.[2] Not only did reform activity addressing sexuality become professionalized through the rise of social work and urban studies, but sexuality itself came under increasing scrutiny from a growing medical and scientific establishment. Sexual practice became indicative of personality and identity in famed scientific analyses. It was a dynamic topic for the finest minds of the day; everyone from Havelock Ellis to Richard von Krafft-Ebing to Sigmund Freud published elaborate treatises on the subject.

The need to produce identity markers was exacerbated by the mass population movements of the late nineteenth and early twentieth century. Millions of southern and eastern Europeans came to America, and millions of native-born white Americans moved from rural to urban settings. Simultaneously, hundreds of thousands of African Americans moved from the South to parts of the North and Midwest. Sexuality and its literal offspring, reproduction, were naturally of great interest to those concerned with the impact of these shifting populations. Consequently, the scientific interest—prurient though it often was—seemed to rest upon a rational basis. Yet the conclusions drawn from these efforts often reflected the embedded limitations of middle-class morality, particularly concerns about social order suffused with class and racial prejudices.

The sexual fears articulated with respect to immigrants and workers in the turn-of-the-century city had deep racial roots. Little was said about workers and immigrants that was not said first about African Americans. According to white southerners, African American men were rapacious sexual predators (when they were not impotent men-children à la Uncle Tom), and African American women were licentious and sexually available. These stereotypes enlisted sexuality as a justification for oppression. Long-standing southern white terror over racial mixing contributed to a growing national ideology that emphasized white purity and decried "race suicide"—a concern that whites were not reproducing as rapidly as immigrants and racial minorities. European immigrants to northern cities found these stereotypes and fears applied to them; one can easily imagine what happened to the large numbers of African Americans who migrated to the same places. These population shifts fundamentally altered the demographic composition of many northern and midwestern cities by 1920, touching off something akin to sexual panic in much of the country. In this context, the Progressive Era obsession with sexuality and the aggressive nature of reform efforts make perfect, if painful, sense.

How did this obsessive interest evolve into modern sexuality? In one sense, the answer is not complicated. The scientific engagement with the subject and the placement of sexuality within a regulatory grid of laws and norms have the ring of modernity to them. The more a subject appears on the public horizon, the more people want to join in the discussion. Surely this is a familiar principle when we think of sexuality. Yet turn-of-the-century discussions about sex were very different from ours. Tracing the development of their world into ours requires us to look carefully at the nuances of these very public conversations.

Some of the details remain cloudy. Although reformer agitation gives us a window onto the complex urban sexual environment of the period in question, we have a less complete picture of what occurred elsewhere. In urban centers unmarried men and women created a flexible sexual structure focusing on personal autonomy and sexual pleasure; women negotiated sexual territories with some degree of confidence, and self-identified homosexual communities flourished in many locales.[3] But did such processes go on in smaller communities whose racial and ethnic makeup had not changed for generations? The answer is a resounding yes. Though supposedly insulated from the sexual chaos endemic to the city, small-town America found itself ensnared in sexual controversies.

This book captures moments from that struggle. The stories illustrate a painful contest over how sexuality would be seen and understood. Local residents and local courts clashed over what constituted acceptable sexual ideology and behavior, and there were no clear-cut winners and losers. The prosecutors tended to win, but often at great cost; communities ultimately did change, but whether for better or worse remains open to debate.

The book includes stories of aggressive sexual play by young women and men who created their own rules but ran afoul of community standards. In many of these cases, though the men were the official defendants, the women found themselves just as much on trial; the abusive words shouted at them stun us with their foreshadowing of a sexual world to come. The people who appeared in these courts violated the sexual rules, which the sources clearly identify. However, something interesting emerges as we look at these records: increasingly, it was the law and the courts that were judged to be in violation of community norms. The community—in the form of juries, witnesses, and even defendants—used the courtroom as a forum to express disagreement and dismay with the statutes governing sexual behavior. These courtroom conflicts became a mechanism that drove the shift in sexual attitudes. When sexual practice appeared before the bar, consternation abounded, and cases often ended in chaos. As individuals talked about their experiences, new values emerged and older ones were shattered. The testimony revealed a world very different from that prescribed in law, and the public nature of these confrontations made these vast discrepancies known to a wide audience.

A large audience did exist for sexual argument and imagery, which is why this book stretches beyond the confines of the county courthouse. It is not enough to look only at court records. Viewed in the absence of the excited discussion in the contemporaneous popular culture, the court records seem almost sterile. And if it is indeed possible that stern court officials were themselves unfamiliar with the popular sentiments that surrounded them, we repeat their mistake at our own peril. Film and vaudeville appeared ubiquitously at the turn of the century, bringing images of a playful sexual culture to audiences throughout the country. This national scope is important, because Progressive Era defenders of public decency (and their later chroniclers) characterized salacious images as strictly urban phenomena. Though it makes little sense to talk about a singular mass culture with a unified sexual sensibility in this period, we can see the beginnings of such a culture (particularly in early film), as well as clues to the methods used in its construction. Films portrayed specific images that helped create new sexual codes. By offering certain sexual stereotypes that fit both the new medium and the concerns of the audience, film contributed significantly to the renegotiation of public sexuality. Its impact fundamentally altered how sexuality was understood and articulated.

Court battles and popular entertainment worked in tandem in turn-of-the-century America, and they do so as well in this book. Sometimes the courts and the popular images reinforced each other; sometimes they stood at odds. Inevitably there emerged between the two a relationship that enriched each set of representations, allowing us to gain a complex understanding of the sexual concerns of the day and of the future. These two often divergent sources offer a front-row seat to pivotal shifts in the history of modern sexuality in America.

This book focuses on apparently settled and unremarkable moments and shows how contested they actually were. Early cinematic representations of female sexual pleasure provided the backdrop for a ferocious argument over appropriate heterosexuality in communities around the country. Simultaneously, testimony about the centrality of sexual desire in the lives of single young women surfaced in statutory rape trials, darkly echoing the lighthearted cinematic imagery. Vaudeville acts celebrating female impersonation delighted theatergoers around the country but raised questions about the relationship between gender and sexual practice. Though audiences everywhere paid for the privilege of being fooled by these elegant deceptions, local communities persecuted male homosexuals, whose similar activities offstage elicited not titillation but fear.

As sexuality among unmarried individuals—both heterosexual and homosexual—became an increasingly contentious subject, attention swung to that supposedly stabilizing force: marriage. Not surprisingly, here, too, sexual disorder reigned. The role of sexuality within marriage inspired controversy on film and in divorce depositions. Husbands and wives jockeyed for sexual power both on screen and in the home, and all found themselves increasingly ensnared in a rhetoric combining commerce and sexuality. Though the development of modern advertising often receives credit for this phenomenon,[4] cinematic pioneers were the first to treat bodies as commodities to be sold on screen. They helped introduce a growing consumer audience to the expanded possibilities of sexual purchase at exactly the moment when Progressive reformers discovered that the traditional business of selling sex—prostitution—had become troublingly ill-defined. As these sexual controversies were settled, modern sexuality as we know it emerged. This book examines both the techniques and the ideologies behind this transformation.

II

The sexual texts under discussion—the films, vaudeville acts, court trials, and divorce depositions—all offer richly layered narratives. After viewing hundreds of films in the Paper Print Collection of the Library of Congress,[5] analyzing close to 300 divorce cases, and reviewing more than 150 sex-crime trials from Sacramento, California, I have selected a representative sample to retell in detail. Although I make no quantitative claims here, these selections stand in well for many others just like them.

Sacramento, California, the primary site of the court archives surveyed in this book, was a classic turn-of-the-century American community. The state capital in an era of (by today's standards) limited government, Sacramento had a population of only 29,000 in 1900. Though hardly a small town, Sacramento paled in size next to the urban areas usually examined by historians of sexuality. Sacramento's population did not keep pace with the more rapidly growing populations of San Francisco, Oakland, or Los Angeles. Sacramento kept its quiet character not only through its own rural emphasis but also because it served as the hub of a network of small farming and mining towns in the Central Valley and the Sierra Nevada foothills. Consequently, Sacramento offered an excellent demographic mix of rural and working-class families.[6] The *Sacramento Bee*, a local paper with influence on state politics, published the news of Lodi, Placerville, and other hamlets alongside local Sacramento news. In fact, there was more news of the region than of Sacramento itself, reflecting the scattered nature of the *Bee*'s readership and areas of interest. These dispersed communities, together with the somewhat plodding Sacramento, provide an important contrast to the usual sites for the history of sexuality. It was not the quick-paced urban center found in the east, nor was it the rapidly industrializing, growing, bustling, turn-of-the-century city which so often fills our imagination of the period. Although Sacramento itself was larger than many towns, it was by no means a major city, and its citizens faced the same conflicts and confusions plaguing people around the country.

The people in Sacramento had several venues at which to enjoy vaudeville and witness the marvels of early film. In this they were hardly unique. Though many scholars have explored early-twentieth-century popular entertainment and its relationship to workers and immigrants in big cities (particularly New York),[7] obviously most Americans lived elsewhere. These primarily white, native-born patrons of vaudeville and film lived far from urban centers, in areas relatively free of immigration. The popular pleasures of stage and screen for these audiences have received less attention. However, a national network of popular entertainment brought big-city sights and sounds across the country, and these programs were not the least shy in addressing sexual topics. The beloved entertainments of small-town America in the first few years of the twentieth century included local melodrama, traveling exhibitors, the latest vitascope offerings, and vaudeville. Few communities were denied the opportunity to witness these migrating delights. Players on competing vaudeville circuits (major ones included Orpheum, Pantages, and Hippodrome) traveled all over the country. From Aberdeen, South Dakota, to Saskatoon, Saskatchewan, to Sacramento, California, locals in small towns and surrounding farm areas had the opportunity to enjoy the same comedies and dramas seen by their more cosmopolitan contemporaries.

Vaudeville and film are often mistakenly thought of as primarily New York phenomena. True, big-time vaudeville *was* based in New York, and performers believed that the pinnacle of success lay there. But the overwhelming majority of vaudeville entertainers, and there were thousands, came from smaller communities around the country and toiled in obscurity on small-time circuits far from New York and from the midwestern vaudeville hub, Chicago. Similarly, although the bulk of early American films came from producers based in New York, many traveled to the far reaches of the country.

Once projection technology in the form of the vitascope replaced the kinescope, a single-viewer machine, in 1896, film exhibition developed somewhat of a "wildcat" quality. Various competing companies produced equipment and films; in fact, the early history of film technology is dominated by corporate intrigue and lawyers' fees.[8] Ultimately there emerged a nationwide network of exhibitors, who operated in whatever venues suited their needs. As film historian Charles Musser notes, when the vitascope exploded onto the scene, it turned up in "any locality large enough to boast an electrical system."[9] Many exhibitors purchased projectors and films and took off for parts still unknown. In 1903, for example, American Mutascope and Biograph had a fire sale on its first films. One distributor bought up many of them and traveled across the country offering small-town theaters a regular supply.[10] Records of such turn-of-the-century entrepreneurs are, needless to say, spotty, but their activity helped fuel public hunger for movies and spread the imagery to the far corners of the country.[11]

Although early film exhibition was associated with, among other things, traveling magic lantern shows and the lecture circuit, its most successful alliance came with vaudeville. The auspicious initial commercial meeting between the two media came on April 23, 1896, when Koster and Bial's Music Hall in New York featured a vitascope program. For the first time, a large audience watched projected film.[12] Immediately, vaudeville operators around the country demanded access to the new entertainment. Until nickelodeon theaters, the small storefront operations that specialized in showing movies for a nickel, emerged around 1907, vaudeville remained the most reliable distribution channel for films.[13] Film historians argue over whether early films were used as "chasers"—boring interludes designed to drive out vaudeville audiences so that new customers could enter—or as exciting additions that promoted film as an entertainment form.[14] Though the relationship between vaudeville and film seems to have had some rocky spots, it cannot be doubted that the expansion of vaudeville to include film benefited both media.

Film distribution records from the period are scanty, so it is not always possible to know precisely where and when films were shown. The fact that we can trace the films more effectively through New York and other major urban centers should not restrict our willingness to assess their potential impact elsewhere. Though exact distribution patterns in more remote areas will remain forever unknown, it is certain that millions of Americans, many in isolated small communities, had the opportunity to watch and respond to moving picture images.[15]

Those images were often paired with vaudeville acts, records of which are very difficult to unearth. When vaudeville entertainers traveled, they adapted. They rarely wrote down the original dialogues, let alone the off-the-cuff remarks or facial expressions. However, we know that reformers perennially critiqued vaudeville as sexually offensive, so it can be surmised that these performances contained a good deal of unrecoverable material that might have helped in this study.

According to standard vaudeville mythology, in 1881 New York music-hall owner Tony Pastor, seeking to expand his audience beyond its traditionally male base, banned smoking and drinking and trumpeted "clean" performances. His success encouraged other New York operators to follow suit, and by 1890 huge audiences were enjoying supposedly family-friendly entertainment: singers, acrobats, comedians, and trained dogs. Edward F. Albee and B. F. Keith emerged as the dominant names in vaudeville production. Playing the "clean house" theme to the hilt, the two entrepreneurs built the largest and most successful vaudeville circuit in the country, setting the standard for would-be challengers. Frederick Proctor and Sylvester Poli established competing circuits in the East, and the Pantages circuit warred with Sullivan and Considine for control of the West as vaudeville established itself as America's most popular national entertainment.[16]

Despite the loud claims of wholesomeness, however, the concept of a cleaned-up vaudeville stage remained slippery. In the course of this research, I surveyed more than twenty years of vaudeville programs and ephemera, and virtually all contained an admonition either to the audience or to the players that the house would "no longer" tolerate offensive behavior. The struggle seems to have been endless; one suspects that historians of vaudeville have taken the Pastors, Proctors, and Keiths too much at their word. It seems likely that vaudeville maintained a significantly suggestive character but that the audience was composed of people whose own sensibility about what constituted offensive material was itself under reconstruction.

Knowing the extent of vaudeville's reach offers us important information about its capacity to transmit sexual imagery. Quantifying the number and location of vaudeville theaters remains a daunting task. The few counts done were performed by contemporary New York trade papers with an eastern bias and an emphasis on circuit theaters in more populated areas. According to these surveys, roughly 400 legitimate vaudeville theaters existed in 1906, and perhaps 2,500 to 5,000 smaller venues often hosted vaudeville acts. When one considers the countless numbers of itinerant film projectionists, the vast array of screening possibilities becomes evident.[17]

This extraordinary network of theaters and gathering places attracted viewers from various classes. In the formal vaudeville houses, a tiered admission system reinforced class stratification, yet it simultaneously broke down barriers by presenting the same material to everyone. Popular entertainment as the great American leveler is a problematic theory. Yet in the search for a modern sexual ethos, one cannot ignore the fact that working-class and middle-class men and women were offered identical sexual representations. How they saw, heard, and interpreted that information would, of course, vary, but that commonality became crucial as sexual metaphor and behavior began to transcend class lines in this period. This transcendence was one important factor paving the way for publicly inclusive articulations of sexuality.

The conclusions drawn in the book are made possible by the national character of popular entertainment in the early twentieth century. It is safe to say that a significant variety of sexual images reached well beyond the big cities to the furthest corners of America. This rich sexual texture could be found throughout the country. Debates over film censorship often took place in smaller communities, reinforcing the perception that these communities had something to "defend" against. As so many of today's politicians attempt to mythologize an innocent, untroubled heartland of the past, they would do well to recall that few places in America were immune from images of sexual confusion and disorder at the turn of the century.

III

I make no attempt to connect all the dots in these stories. We cannot really know whether Charles Harlan ever saw the films described here. But cultural forces do not operate in such a narrow fashion, and if we required that degree of specificity we would miss the larger point. A vast array of sexual images permeated turn-of-the-century American culture at the very moment that shifts in sexual attitudes, both subtle and striking, found voice in local communities. To address one forum without addressing the other would be intentionally to blind oneself to how the sexual world of the early twentieth century really looked to most Americans.

To make sense of this sexual world, this book uses an interpretive strategy highly influenced by cultural studies. The analytic tools provided by these disciplines enable us to reach beyond the bounds of traditional historical problems. Film studies focusing on spectatorship have proved particularly valuable. Though the central debates of that field are by no means the preoccupation of this study, the concepts underlying some of those debates have been applied to these sources, and the interpretive implications may offer some insights to more specialized researchers.

Theories of spectatorship focus on the relationship between what appears on the screen and the viewer. Such theories evolved over several decades. The discussion used to be driven predominantly by psychoanalytic theory, but more recent work has incorporated historical detail. Early theorists posited that the moving image, playing in a darkened space set off from the rest of the world, struck a chord with viewers' internal psychic structures. The audience was drawn into the film metaphorically through identification with the onscreen image. Feminist critics soon noted that, given what appeared on the screen, the "ideal" viewer must inevitably be positioned as male. Subsequent theorists overturned this assumption by arguing that the spectator's sex did not determine his or her understanding of the screen image; cinematic imagery, they claimed, actually invited a fluid set of possible spectator identifications. Using psychoanalytic theory, some asserted that notions of "masculine" and "feminine" float somewhat confusedly in our psyches and surface in complicated ways. Other scholars attempted to determine the social conditions under which actual viewers received the image, then extrapolated a variety of possible spectator relationships.[18] Much of this work has focused on early film spectatorship, and both of these streams of thought have deeply influenced me.

Challenges to the idea of a single spectator position and a dominant cinematic ideology are joined by a growing recognition that film was not such a singular novelty when it emerged. Rather, it appeared from within a series of shifts in material culture and technology that altered the nature of all things visual. Seeing may have always been believing, in the words of countless country philosophers, but what viewers saw and how they saw it could now be managed with extraordinary cleverness and artifice. Shrewdly produced visual spectacles got credit for being real—a rather astonishing leap of faith. The shift from watching the cow in the field, to looking at the photograph of the cow, to viewing the film of the cow walking across the field—all the while "seeing" the same cow—is a dramatic one. As the nineteenth century progressed, people began to "see" their world in a variety of arrangements: elaborate panoramas and dioramas, complicated magic lantern and slide shows, the newly developed department store window, and, of course, early film.

No one really argues that people lacked the capacity to understand that these images were products of technology. Indeed, that very recognition—the "gee whiz" quality—was part of what drew audiences. These attractions set up a new sequence of relationships among the producer of the image, the image itself, and the spectator. Although film ultimately became the primary focus of this multilayered relationship, initially it competed with many other types of imagery. Placing film within this broader context of visual reorientation creates important bridges between cultural theory and historical investigation.

Such bridges helped to undergird the methodology used in this study. The book analyzes both the popular culture and the court cases with an eye toward potential multiple "readings" by their respective "audiences." For example, the court cases have been unearthed not in order to document a distinct social history of sexual prosecutions but rather for their language and imagery—not unlike the films or vaudeville that often accompany them. They are evidence of a sexual culture, representations competing for primacy in the American imagination. In each case, the audience is more wide-ranging than might be otherwise thought. Cinema did not exist in some static form only to produce solitary moments of private pleasure; courtroom representations governing sexuality did not lie dormant in cold transcript files. They became community events with ultimately far-flung community audiences, and they yield a rich picture of a complicated sexual culture with numerous points of view. Many of those perspectives rested upon the growing need for visual imagery, and the impact of this new insistence upon public sexual culture cannot be overestimated.

In 1903, cameraman G. W. Bitzer (who shall reappear often in these pages) filmed a scene entitled "Pulling Off the Bed Clothes."[19] In it, a young scamp rigs the sheets of a bed in one apartment with a string that snakes its way into the next apartment via a transom. He ties the string to the door handle of the adjoining flat. Eventually a woman climbs into the bed, and a moment later a gentleman walks through the booby-trapped entrance. The blankets and sheets fly off the bed, leaving the poor woman exposed and outraged. The film ends there—the scamp is gone, but we are left behind as witnesses. In the following pages, many more bedclothes will come off (hopefully with greater respect), and we will witness moments in the development of a sexual culture whose exceedingly public nature has outraged many. In the process we will gain a more nuanced understanding of an earlier sexual era and greater insight into the roots of our own.

Chapter Two

The Adjustable Bed

Turn-of-the-century America witnessed a dramatic shift in gender relations. The Victorian world of homosocial relationships gradually gave way to one of heterosocial associations. American men and women have always socialized in some fashion; however, such connections—particularly among unmarried individuals—were closely regulated in the nineteenth century, an era of gender-segregated friendships and social networks. Though such networks survive to a degree in today's world, they retain but a shadow of their former substance. The complex, insular nature of those connections withered a century ago under pressure from a new sexual culture that reinforced the idea that men and women should be playmates together.[1]

The sexual dangers of such new social alliances were readily apparent, and Progressive reform activity aimed at vice can be seen in this context. Yet the "obvious" problems over which the Progressives hyperventilated had less dramatic social consequences than did the infinitely more private renegotiations of sexual expectation that occurred between men and women as they came to depend upon each other for social affirmation as well as sexual connection. Though playful sexuality provided the underpinnings for a form of parity between men and women, it introduced troubling anxiety as well. If women were no longer to act as Cerberus, guarding the gates to the sexual hell ever present in unleashed male lust, but instead were to be equal partners in the creation of a sexual understanding, how would the rules be made? How were the boundaries to be drawn? As female desire became incorporated into the popular and private visions of sexual morality at the turn of the century, both men and women confronted a world in flux.

Such questions frame many of the sexual representations found in court documents and early film. These representations sketched a blueprint for appropriate expressions of heterosexual desire. Fears of unacceptable heterosexual practice and even deeper anxieties over what might be termed "anti-heterosexual" practice occupied an important place in the subtext of early film. Similarly, in responding to cases of statutory rape, communities attempted (with mixed success) to agree upon and articulate appropriate heterosexuality. Disagreement surfaced often, and a close reading of testimony uncovers sharp echoes of the cinematic discourses. Together, the films and the trials help illuminate the specific boundaries of and resistances to public heterosexuality. The contest was not won or lost in these early years but continued as an ongoing struggle with rising tides and receding influences.[2]

I

From the inception of film until the rise of serious censorship, a period encompassing the years 1896 to 1910, motion pictures demonstrated a surprising recognition of female desire and sexual availability. This vision of aggressive female sexuality often dominated early short films. In response to such imagery, Progressive reformers came to see movies as a powerful new threat to morality. Film pioneer D. W. Griffith, talented though he may have been, gained enormous support by offering films that reinforced earlier traditions of sexual and personal morality and fought the tide of what many perceived to be amoral movies.[3]

The variety of sexual behavior deemed appropriate in early films is particularly striking. No single moral vision predominated; sexuality remained an uncharted area open to exploration. The territory remained unmapped, the "proper" path not yet set. It is not simply that individual filmmakers and production companies created iconoclastic imagery to match their own sensibilities; rather, a full range of sexual imagery often appeared within the films of a single company or director.

The cinema of this era was a world at play, and filmmakers very often played by depicting sexuality.

The first filmmakers explored a variety of questions that both reflected and ultimately helped shape heterosexual practice among unmarried people. Were women dominant or submissive? Holders of virtue or eager participants in sexual desire? Did male desire constitute inappropriate lechery or youthful pleasure? Could the public enjoy images of desire without transgressing earlier boundaries of moral tradition? Through these explorations—admittedly undertaken by a small number of men—a newly public heterosexual ethic emerged, subtly defining the limits of the possible and the expanse of the unacceptable.

One very popular and influential arena of sexual definition appeared in films that deployed a dominant female stereotype—the frustrated old maid. The image so sharply etched in traditional nineteenth-century wit reappeared in a series of movies that mocked unwed women. Numerous performers and filmmakers built their careers on this imagery, so its cultural power at the turn of the century needs to be assessed with some care.

Gilbert Saroni, perhaps the most famous "old maid" in vaudeville, repeated his act for Edison Film in two separate shorts produced on March 1, 1901: "The Old Maid Having Her Picture Taken"[4] and "The Old Maid in the Horsecar."[5] "The Old Maid Having Her Picture Taken" offered a woman with haggard features and a sharp hook nose. She is notably more skinny and angular than women depicted in other films. The character has large puffy sleeves that look absurd when compared with the costumes worn by younger women in these films, and she carries the requisite fan, which can be used to indicate modesty or distress as needed.

The joke in "The Old Maid Having Her Picture Taken" revolves around the potency of her ugliness. Her countenance has remarkable destructive power. As she enters the room and surveys the wall hangings, they all drop to the floor; the mirror cracks as she primps before the photo session; and, naturally enough, the camera explodes when it is focused upon her. To modern eyes, it looks like an old joke, and no doubt it echoed with familiarity in 1901 as well. That familiarity is precisely the mechanism by which we are able to identify the woman as a sexual—or, in this case, asexual—icon. "The Old Maid in the Horsecar" had no discernible plot, but it reinforced the stereotype through dress and physical presentation. Saroni added a large mole to each cheek, exaggerated his character's long, unkempt ringlets of hair, and occasionally hid his face behind an open fan, seemingly giggling to exhibit a mock girlishness. The image alone provides a certain degree of humor, as does the juxtaposition of the old, broken-down figure and the new, modern conveyance.

American Mutascope and Biograph found the picture-taking scenario sufficiently popular to remake the film in 1903. "The Old Maid's Picture"[6] streamlined the plot to get right to the heart of the joke. Gone were the supplemental signs of disaster; only the primary one—the camera blowing up—remained, ending the picture. Yet the imagery was roughly the same as in the Edison shorts. The old maid is still haggard, though in this version she wears white rather than the more standard black. Her primping for the session is again a primary focus for the humor prior to the camera's exploding. In both films, the explosion knocks the old maid off her feet, leaving her body in a humiliating position, her undergarments exposed to view.

Similar old maid films of the period employ identical female imagery to convey a variety of physical and emotional jokes.[7] All involve rejection of the old maid, whether by objects or by people. The dominating ridicule of this character indicates a socially agreed-upon repudiation of a certain form of older single woman. She stands as an icon of unacceptability—repelled and repellent.

Such imagery demarcated the boundaries of both male and female desire. In her primping, preening, and failed girlish attributes, she attempts to express female attractiveness and be worthy of male sexual attention. Both the use of the fan as facial cover and the prohibitive dress (usually the forbidding black but on occasion the virginal white, in derisive reference to chastity) fostered ridicule of female innocence and sexual inaccessibility. The old maid represented a vision of female desire but also set limits on the type of woman who could appropriately exercise it.

One of the best examples in this genre, "The Disappointed Old Maid," tackled frustrated sexuality directly in 1903.[8] As the film opens, a man dressed in black enters a bedroom through an unlatched window and crawls under the bed. An old maid in white nightclothes enters the room and begins to remove her shoes. As she leans over to do so, she sees the man under her bed. Clapping her hands together in delight, she smiles broadly and dances to the window in order to lock it and trap him inside. She reaches under the bed to pull him out but finds that he is only a large doll. As the film ends, she sits on the bed and cries, cradling the doll in her arms. Lacking in any subtlety whatsoever, "The Disappointed Old Maid" elevates the subtext of the old maid imagery to the surface and confronts it directly. These are women who wish to be sexual actors but are locked out of the world of desire. Men are incapable of feeling desire for them. In fact, in order to truly capture their lack of female sexual appeal, the old maid was best played by a man or made up to look like one.

That the ugly crack mirrors upon sight may be a long-standing cultural joke, but the notion of who constitutes the category of the unsightly is a changing sensibility. The old maid as specifically formulated in turn-of-the-century popular culture was a relatively recent construction, a response to an actual increase in the number of older single women and to the popular identification of such women with the women's rights movement. Both the demographic and the political aspects of the stereotype had some basis in truth. The 1890 and 1900 censuses did reflect significant increases in the number of women who never married, with a particularly high rate of nonmarriage among educated white women.[9] Though not all college women supported suffrage and other feminist causes, many did—and all came to be tarred with the women's-rights brush.

Women who did not marry incurred political and social scorn for another reason. The influx of eastern and southern European immigrants in the United States pushed the question into eugenic terms—the wrong people were reproducing. Educated women came primarily from white middle- and upper-class stock, the most desired element by dominant social norms. When these women refused to marry and reproduce, they forced a new concern into the public discourse.[10] It is not a coincidence that the stereotypical asexual unmarried older woman emerged at this time as a source of popular humor. Antecedents for the physical image of the severe old maid appeared in British dance-hall "dame" caricatures a generation earlier[11] and, perhaps more significant for American cultural iconography, in representations of witches stemming from the eighteenth and nineteenth centuries. Just as witches in earlier cultural incarnations had represented, at least partially, sexuality out of control,[12] the old maid symbolized sexuality unused and thus outside of communal control and direction.

This is a figure who resists heterosexuality as constructed in the early twentieth century. A sneering popular culture specifically targeted women's-rights advocates, tainting them as perverted or "barren," thus delimiting heterosexuality even more boldly.[13] If the Gilbert Saroni figure carried no banners, the joke was nevertheless understood. This character type represented female resistance to heterosexuality. Yet even as it helped to scorn this figure, early film indicated the level of anxiety she produced.

However, the old maid imagery served more than one master. The derision of wasted sexual potential betrayed a recognition of desire—useful, appropriate, or otherwise. As the mocking discourse grew, a counterdiscourse followed that incorporated female desire into a vision of normative sexual activity. The old maid warned women of the danger of thwarted desire and acted as an outer boundary to an emerging sexual sensibility; in a sense, she represented a photographic negative of appropriate female sexuality. In the emphatic dismissal of the old maid, we can also readily view an invitation to women to enter a public sexual dialogue previously reserved for males. This invitation may indeed have been a necessary response to a perceived increase in female resistance to heterosexual imperatives.

The proposition surfaces in early Edison and Biograph films that both reflected and provided models for a world of sexually engaged men *and* women. Many of the movies are remarkable in showing not only the sexual possibilities available to women but also the responsibility for initiation often placed upon them. Though some of this sexuality seems to be reserved for women characterized as wanton, much of it is not. Many "respectable" female characters find themselves happily ensconced in entanglements reflecting their own sexual desire. The images created an impression of active female sexuality and helped to establish women as agents of desire. This encompassing vision represents an important shift in cultural imagination, giving us a window on a critical moment in the history of sexual values.

Many turn-of-the-century filmmakers used actual windows to create a panorama of sexual action. With their immutable boundaries, open windows and doorways offered experimental frames within a frame, tailor-made for artistic conceptualizations. In one of the best-known early films, "What Demoralized the Barbershop" (made twice by Edison),[14] the barbershop, a basement establishment of male privacy and prerogative, is thrown into an uproar at the sight of striped stockings worn by women walking past the street-level front door. Everyone in the shop reacts. The man getting his shoes shined won't sit still; the barber cranes his head to catch a glance and carelessly whips his huge razor across a squirming and screaming customer. Patrons knock things over trying to get a better look. The women are not unaware of the commotion they are causing; they stop at the doorway, lift their skirts, and show their legs through the open framed area over the men's heads.

Though such shenanigans seem tame by today's standards, these 1898 and 1901 productions lent early witness to the public dialogue on sexuality—particularly as it concerned male lust and female purity. In contradiction to the Progressive rhetoric about rapacious men, lust here is portrayed as a form of bumbling impotence that might wreak havoc inside the sanctuary of male isolation but otherwise poses little threat. The imagery of female instigation belonged to an ongoing counterdiscourse to reformer ideology which blamed male lechery on female wantonness.

There is little within the film to indicate anything about the character or class of the young ladies. Most films about disreputable young women made their low status quite plain. Here, status is not at issue; the humor comes from the recognition that these men are flustered by their sexual arousal at a "glimpse of stocking" and from the knowledge that the girls who wear those stockings are deliberately attempting to disrupt the male psyche. During this era the concept was sufficiently new to public discourse that the joke could emerge from the reversal of standard attitudes. Though this reversal humor would hold sway for several more years, the change in attitudes reflected in "What Demoralized the Barbershop" had now begun in earnest.

By 1905, when American Mutascope and Biograph made its own barbershop film, "The Barber's Dee-Light,"[15] the Edison version and its underlying humor were sufficiently familiar that they could be satirized. Instead of a single doorway, this basement has a series of sidewalk-level windows in the upper quarter. The men watch delightedly as women walk past. These customers seem more in control of themselves than the men in the earlier versions, and they hold the power, directing their sexual gazes at presumably unknowing passersby. Finally the prerequisite skirt and stockinged legs fill the doorway. Playing on the public's familiarity with "What Demoralized the Barbershop," filmmaker G. W. Bitzer has the legs stop in the doorway and then begin to turn and come down into the barbershop. The parameters had been sufficiently stretched by 1905 that a female's visual presence alone is insufficient to create the boundary transgression from which the humor derives. Physical entry into male enclave is necessary. But Bitzer improves on the joke. As the stockinged legs come down the stairs, they turn out to belong to a foppish man in tights with a flowing cape and a decidedly effeminate manner. The barbershop customers are shocked and discombobulated. In this clever cinematic turn, Bitzer transgressed several boundaries simultaneously, raising the ever-present concern over gender identities and how they could be properly defined.[16]

Popular artists exploring sexual expression saw the female body as more than a skirt and a pair of legs. The body took on a specific physical reality, almost as a counter to the ethereal vision of the Victorian woman. Here, the movies clearly reflected a growing cultural trend that encouraged women to exercise and to see their bodies as a natural part of themselves instead of as an "animal" side to be shunned. Doctors and educators in the late nineteenth century began to reject the prevailing medical view that physical activity was debilitating for middle- and upper-class women. Instead, physicians began to encourage women to engage in exercise and recreational activity. The debate over proper physical activity often centered on issues that were either openly or covertly sexual. Bicycle riding, for example, was a source of much controversy, as was swimming. Despite the argument, "physical culture," as it was called, became quite a rage among young women of the upper classes.[17]

The connection between physical culture and a woman's capacity to take care of herself in the battle for sexual parity appeared often in

films of the period. Numerous works satirized the craze and placed it
in a sexual context. "The Physical Culture Lesson," made in 1906 by
G. W. Bitzer (probably the most prolific early filmmaker),[18] takes the
otherwise unstated sexual potential and makes it explicit. A dark-
suited man comes to give a young lady her calisthenics lesson. They
seem to be in the dressing area of her home. As the instructor
demonstrates each exercise, his pupil only replicates it partially, con-
tinually forcing him to reach over and guide her body with his hands.
When she does a leg lift, he grabs her ankle and pulls it upward, exaggerating the movement. She primps at the dressing table in between exercises. At the end of the lesson, he sits down to rest, and
she is pulled onto his lap. The film ends with them kissing as she sits
on his lap.

Bitzer's fascination with sex and exercise also appeared in "The
Athletic Girl and the Burglar," a short comedy from 1905.[19] The title
describes the plot, although both versions submitted to the Library of
Congress for copyright also flirt with the suggestion of rape. Though
Bitzer's athletic girls were generally shapely and pretty by the standards of the period, the actress here was larger, older, and clearly intended to be perceived as less than attractive. In one version she enters a room with gym equipment, takes off her hat and coat, and
begins to work with the wall pulleys and barbells. She lies down to
continue her workout, and while she is in that position a man in
scruffy clothing sneaks up on her. She stops exercising, beats him up
with the barbells, and returns to her activities. The second version, of
which only half as much film remains, is a bit more risqué. The
woman enters a bedroom and removes her blouse and skirt, leaving
only her undergarments. She is on the floor doing leg lifts when the
burglar enters. Their struggle is more physical, as he tries to slug her
before she knocks him out with the barbell. She then continues doing
her calisthenics, unfazed.

Images of female athleticism provided erotic representations because they placed women's bodies on display in a fashion that implied
sexual access. Bitzer recognized and satirized that fact. His films on
the subject simply showed the new phenomenon in all its startling ir-
regularity.[20] These first efforts seem to have served as some form of
soft pornography; they are well in line with a number of films whose

sole purpose was to show women engaging in some form of physical action in inappropriate, often suggestive clothing.[21] By adding a specific sexual subtext through the plot, Bitzer reinforced an emerging public vision of a female body available to male desire. Moreover, women were eager participants in the creation and consumption of these images, skewed though they might be. The images were not intended exclusively for the rarefied world of private male lust but were instead aimed at the culture at large, becoming part of the free-floating, unfettered social dialogue on relations between men and women. Women as well as men were to be in on the joke. The assumption that women would understand humor of such a sexual nature presupposes a fundamental recognition that women were engaged in the sexual dialogue. The films discussed here thus indicate shifts in both focus and audience.

The women and men viewing these short comedies could happily share responsibility for sexual encounters and enjoy the effects together. In early examples of what would become standard silent-movie bits for the next generation, films such as "Love in a Hammock," "Three Girls in a Hammock," "The Adjustable Bed," and "Always Room for One More,"[22] all released by 1905, created their humor by having men and women attempt to occupy too small or too fragile a physical space at the same time. Inevitably collapsing on top of each other, the characters always ended up laughing, embracing, and kissing. Filmmakers presented physicality and sexuality as both entertaining for witnesses and fun for participants. In so doing, they both responded to emerging sentiments and helped propel them forward.

Early film presented surprisingly subtle and fascinating rearticulations not only of heterosexuality but also of its subversion. Images of resistance to heterosexuality (such as the old maid) contain the seeds of both cultural anxiety and, because the character is contained on screen, social recuperation. Many of these early representations draw sharp boundaries to male and female heterosexual practice. Early film conveyed to viewers a clear, albeit complex, understanding of what constituted appropriate sexual play for single men and women. Although presented through the lens of male fantasy, these films offered an expanded sexual vision to women as well. The fantasy may have been designed for male pleasure, but its fulfillment might easily occur in the hearts and minds of female viewers.

II

Yet the films did not exist in a world without tradition. The representations captured in these movies did not stand as the final statement of some "new" sexuality. Rather, they were attempts to reformulate existing public understandings governing heterosexuality. This evolution appeared clearly on the screen and could be heard with equal ferocity in the arena of public conflict. In the world as on the screen, women came to be incorporated into a vision of desire and lust, both as objects and as participants. This transformation brought costs as well as pleasures, both for individuals unsure of the rules and for a society facing an uncertain future.

The uncertainty played out in personal relations throughout the country. Though audiences may have delighted in the sexual hijinks of popular entertainment, they were not merely passive observers. Many viewers struggled in their own lives to negotiate a path through the tangled emotional thickets of the changing sexual ethos. Testimony and court documents from statutory rape trials in Sacramento, California, demonstrate that determining the rules for sexual activity was no easy matter at the turn of the century.[23] In these proceedings we find a besieged traditional order trying with mixed success to shore up a waning moral and sexual ethic. Simultaneously, the records illustrate a readjustment of sexual values among those accused of misconduct as well as among their prosecutors and judges. The hard-working farmers and railroad employees who composed local juries did not decide cases of sexual transgression by applying a simple moral equation. Guilt and innocence in such matters became increasingly difficult to recognize. As early-twentieth-century court records show, men and women in Sacramento began to express their confusion and a desire to alter the terms of the conversation that governed sexual relations. These sentiments resonated from the voices of both those who sought to challenge existing rules and those who would uphold them.

The trial of Antonio Kuches illustrates this confusion well. The case contained many theatrical elements as well as an unconventional—and discomfiting—defense. Kuches, a thirty-year-old immigrant candy-store clerk, faced a charge of assault with intent to rape in 1896. Local child protective officer Dan Healy accused him of taking fourteen-year-old Emma Metz into the back room of his candy store and attempting to have intercourse with her. Officer Healy burst in on the scene shortly after Kuches pulled out his penis but before he could pull up Metz's skirt. (Healy's remarkable timing fills Sacramento court files, and one wonders whether he regularly lied or merely lurked everywhere.) However, Kuches and his local attorney, D. E. Alexander, presented very disquieting testimony about would-be victim Metz. The defendant's shocking tale of Metz's forward conduct was obviously suspect, but its detail and assumptions reflected a disturbingly different vision of sexual play from what jurors might have expected or wanted to hear:

I asked her what she wanted, and she slapped me in the face and laughed. I never touched her. . . . She as much as told me to take it. . . . I says, 'What do you want?' . . . she continued to fool around with me laughing all the time. . . . I was scared for fear she was too small. . . . she threw hints at me just as much as to say you can have it and I thought she was too small. . . . Then with that she opened her drawers. She started to laugh and she sat down on the chair and I touched her on the cheek. She slapped my face and started to laugh, and I started to say something and touched her on the breast, and with that she started to open her pants, and she was ready to take it.[24]

Though such testimony can be dismissed as self-serving, Kuches was hardly alone in characterizing Metz as a sexual flirt. Sixteen-year-old Charles Strathmeyer, who had played and worked with Metz since they were small children, provided ample supporting evidence. Although the judge denied the defense's request to present Strathmeyer's testimony that Emma "continuously indulged in the telling of dirty and smutty stories and continuously was propounding riddles that were vulgar and indecent,"[25] Strathmeyer and some of his friends did make other damning revelations on the witness stand. They told the story of the day they all went to pick hops and Metz asked for help. Sixteen-year-old Gilmer Holmes testified that Strathmeyer

wanted to know "what will you give me," and that when Metz's
brother came upon them she "was lying on her back and Strathmeyer
was going to get on top of her."[26] Willie Cotter said, "Strathmeyer
went down with her to the field to do it to her."[27] Strathmeyer himself
disclosed how "she laid down on her back and was taking her pants
down and just then her brother came. . . . She laid down there and I
was going to get on top of her; she asked me to go down there with
her, she was perfectly willing at that time. . . . she told me to come
down and she would give me something."[28] One final witness denied
that Metz's brother arrived on the scene by accident: "He was on to
the proposition. Her brother made a sneak around so as to catch
them. He knew what they were up to; we all knew what they were up
to. It was all understood that they were all to get something for picking hops for her."[29]

The defense pleaded with the jury and judge to see Emma Metz as
a participant and not a victim. They requested a jury instruction quite
remarkable for its day: "Her body is at her own disposal and she is ca-
pable of assenting to acts of sexual intercourse and her conduct is to
be judged in exactly the same light that you would judge the conduct
of an older woman."[30] The judge accepted the bulk of the request,
changing the final clause to "in light of all the circumstances surrounding the case."[31]

The jury was not swayed, and the foreigner Kuches received ten
years in prison. Perhaps the jury dismissed the testimony concerning
Emma Metz's past not because it seemed obviously false or self-
serving but rather because it sounded frighteningly possible. If today
such comments would represent an obvious defense ploy, in 1896 jurors might consider them outrageous insults to the character of a "little girl." Yet that "girl" had been working quite independently in the
community as a department-store clerk and itinerant farm laborer for
some time. Hers had been a childhood filled with autonomy and a
strong whiff of independent sexual behavior.

Alexander's closing plea stands out as both prescient and insight-
ful—a vision of a present under reevaluation and a rapidly unfolding
future. Though the defense attorney may have believed a woman's
body to be at her own disposal merely as a way to win an acquittal for
a client, he nevertheless captured with stunning accuracy both the

emerging image of female sexuality reflected in turn-of-the-century popular culture and the essence of what we know as "modern" sexuality. The call to the jury explicitly presumed the existence of female desire, even among younger women, and its bold assumption that women owned their own bodies crossed barriers of age and spoke directly to a new generation. Even as the jurors rejected Kuches's story, they were forced into a public reevaluation of how men and women expressed and negotiated sexual desires. Even if all the witnesses lied about Emma Metz, they did not fundamentally lie about an existing code of sexual conduct. Aggressive flirtation, rowdy humor, and exchanged sexual favors were clearly not limited to the working-class youth of New York or Chicago.

This direct, dynamic testimony, given in an 1896 Sacramento courtroom, confirmed that the changes encoded in the growing mass culture did not necessarily filter down to the smaller communities. The evidence contradicts a "trickle down" theory of urban licentiousness polluting small towns and rural areas through the popularization of big-city culture. Sacramento and smaller communities faced their own undercurrent of sexual transformation, which mirrored developments in urban America. Rather than merely being changed by the film and stage images that passed through their towns, residents in these communities undoubtedly identified with these images, finding them familiar and relevant to their own sensibilities and concerns. In this context, the enormous popularity of early movies on the small-time circuit appears to reflect a process of reaffirmation rather than of indoctrination.

Still, 1896 is early in this transformation of public heterosexuality. Though the timing makes the defense remarks in the Kuches trial all the more fascinating, it would be unfair to imply that changes occurred easily or without a struggle among the contending social forces. As films soared in popularity during the first decade of the twentieth century, the private debate, as seen in the trials of young men accused of sexual crimes, roared fiercely. The gravity of those cases contrasted sharply with the lighthearted sexual humor presented by the films. Sexual negotiations may have seemed funny on screen, but to communities in transition the evidence of similar activity in their hometowns forced crises of moral order that often resulted in palpable rage.

Fourteen-year-old Almary Jones felt the full force of that rage after she began meeting John Salle secretly during the dog days of a Sacramento October in 1910. The rules for sexual behavior had become cloudy, and judgments about that behavior were difficult to make. Everyone testifying at the grand jury indictment for rape against Salle, a twenty-five-year-old Southern Pacific boiler-shop worker, had recognized that his involvement with Jones might cause trouble, and all claimed to have warned him. Salle acknowledged that although he thought Jones looked about sixteen, he suspected that she was younger. Salle pled guilty, and when he was finally sentenced to five years in prison it was agreed that a deservedly light punishment had been handed down.[32]

Great sympathy was expressed for Salle, reflecting the confusion felt by the community. Even the judge, who seemed determined to assign blame away from the "little girl" in question, found Salle troublingly respectable: "This young man . . . is an earnest, hard worker. Everyone of his co-employees in the shops, where he works, speak well of him; many testified in the trial of those who were associated with him in the commission of this offense, and all spoke of the defendant as a hard working, good boy."[33] His attorney pleaded with the court that "he is not a criminal. There is not anything criminal in him. From the first arrest of this young man up to the present moment, his conduct has been that of an exemplary, honest, straightforward young fellow."[34] Reluctantly, the judge denied a defense request for probation and sentenced the defendant to prison, but those who bore witness agreed with Salle's attorney, who argued that "the circumstances surrounding his guilt should appeal to the manhood of every man here who hears his story."[35]

Those circumstances reflected the private life of many such young men and women, including the dozens who testified in Salle's behalf. Salle and his friends played together in ways unfamiliar to a staid legal system that did not quite know what to do with them. Their play was energetic and engaged. It rested on a mutuality of interest between men and women and assumed at its base an understanding and acceptance of desire. The judge may have seen a "pretty little girl in short dresses to the knees . . . attending the primary school"[36] when he looked at Almary Jones, but Salle and friends from both camps knew her as an independent young woman with more than a little sexual experience to guide her through relations with her new beau. All the differing impressions were true. John Salle was just as respectable as he seemed to be, and yet not so; Almary Jones was both innocent and "wild." In this they were much like their friends, and it is clear, as we read the text of this case, that neither Almary nor John was anybody special at all.

They met at a Saturday night dance, a regular weekly event that brought out people of a variety of ages and types. Almary had been brought by her mother on occasion. Julia Jones, a deserted wife, struggled to make a living for her five children, working all day and taking in boarders. She and a daughter-in-law accompanied Almary on several Saturdays to relax at this respectable, locally sponsored entertainment. The chaperoned dances at Turner Hall were considered a safe way for young people to meet each other. Almary, accompanied by her mother and friends, had every reason to know that this was proper behavior.

When she went to the dance for several weeks with one of her mother's female boarders, however, the stakes got a little higher. Almary and Mabel Springer found in each other the support they needed to explore their own sexual potential. Mabel and her husband, Morris, an independent roofer, lived at the Jones home in the summer and fall of 1910. She and Almary became friends and began to go to the Saturday night dances without Mrs. Jones. Almary met John Salle and his boiler-shop buddy Pete Kostena and then introduced them to Mabel Springer. Mabel paired off with Pete, and Almary joined up with John. Following the dance, the four went to the Eagle, a local restaurant catering to working-class patrons. They had some supper and a few beers (the grand jury was stunned to learn that the young Almary drank real lager, or, as she called it, "Bohemian Beer"),[37] finally getting home at 1:30 A.M.

During the week Salle sent Jones a cryptic postcard urging the women to meet him and Pete at the corner of Seventh and K Streets at 8:00 P.M. on Thursday night. The four went to the theater, then to the Eagle, and then took a stroll through Capitol Park, the extensive and beautiful grounds surrounding the State Capitol. Almary and John lay in the grass, fondling and kissing, but when John said he wanted to "fuck," she put him off by telling him that she was "sick" with her "monthlies."[38] They met again, by the same method, the next week. That evening, after going to the movies and making the requisite midnight visit to the Eagle, they decided to get a room. While still at the restaurant, Mabel spoke to Almary in the bathroom: "I told her that Kostena promised me ten dollars if I would stay with him, and she said she would stay also. I told her she hadn't better. She better go home . . . She said she was going anyway. She said if Mr. Salle would give her some money, she would go; but she liked Pete [*sic*; corrected testimony to "John"], and she would go anyway."[39] Mabel gave Almary advice on how to wash herself afterward, and the four took off in search of rooms. It was no small task. Three or four rooming houses turned them away. They finally found two basement rooms a few blocks from the Eagle.

An extremely reluctant witness, Almary testified about what happened next. Earlier, she apparently had given a comprehensive statement to the district attorney, but Almary now infuriated the grand jury by refusing to give detailed answers.

Q: Well, now just what did he do? What sort of object did he put into you? What was the shape of it? Take your hand down from your mouth and the quicker you tell, the better. What was the shape of the object he put into you? Was it square?

A: No sir.

Q: Well, what was the shape? Do you know what it is called?

A: No sir.

Q: Well, if it was not square, what was the shape of it?

A: Round.

Q: Was it hard or soft?

A: Soft, I guess.

Q: Well, don't you know? Was it hard or soft? Well, whereabouts did he put it into you? What portion of you? Were you lying on your stomach or on your back?

A: Back.

Q: What portion of your body did he put that into you? Did he put it into any opening on your body?

A: Yes sir.

Q: What do you use that opening for? Do you know what organ you use
        when you go to the toilet to pass water?

A: Yes sir.

Q: Was that the place he put the organ into you?

A: No sir.[40]

Exasperated, the interrogator began to badger her even further,
demanding to know why she was refusing to answer questions and
whether anyone had spoken to her about the case or was cajoling her
to marry Salle. She finally acknowledged that he had put the organ
into the center of the opening between her legs. The jury then demanded to know the details of the penetration.

Q: How much of it was put inside you, do you know?

A: No sir.

Q: Well, can you tell anything how much? Was it an inch or two inches
        or half an inch?

A: An inch, I guess.

Q: Did you feel anything inside of you when he was in that position on
        top of you? Answer the question. Did you feel anything inside of you
        when he was on top of you?

A: I felt it.[41]

The jury harassed her mercilessly for quite some time longer,
eventually getting her to spell out letter by letter ("f-u-c-k") the word
Salle had used to describe their activity and finally to confess that she
had told Salle that she was sixteen.

The Foreman: What was your idea in telling him that you were sixteen
                 when you were only fourteen? Did you have some object
                 in telling him that?

       A: No sir.[42]

Salle had contacted her by mail once again after the evening in
question. The four met up by the saloon at Seventh and K, where the
three adults were arrested and Almary was sent to a detention home.
The records do not indicate how they came to be discovered, but

since the four were less than subtle in their movements and remained within four blocks of the Jones home at all times, it is likely that someone brought the situation to the attention of Julia Jones.[43]

The case troubled the community because innocence and guilt played little part. Though the case clearly fell within the legal definition of statutory rape, the jury had no stomach to convict. Within three or four years, almost all such cases of consensual activity would routinely result in probation for the man in question. The law, however, took time to catch up with society; in 1910, such flaunted sexual independence still remained within a context of criminality.

Yet assigning criminal responsibility was not the jury's only intent. The extensive questioning of Jones about the specifics of penetration was clearly meant to be a form of punishment. The law demanded that penetration be established for the case to be classified as statutory rape, so the questions may have been inevitable. But Salle, in his statement to the district attorney, had already confessed to having intercourse with Jones, making the questioning of Jones seem gratuitous. Further, the tone of the interrogation was stunningly assaultive. The grand jurors were enraged at Jones and used their power to humiliate her. They could see that her reluctance to testify did not reflect the shyness of a child, as they might have wished. Rather, the details of the case made readily apparent that Almary Jones knew the score. She also understood that these men were *her* prosecutors, not her protectors. Her refusal to respond seems to have been precisely what they thought it was, a willful rejection of their authority and a concern for her own "guilty" neck.

Almary Jones's decision to go on secret dates with John Salle reflected her own sexual sensibility. Though her court testimony was vague as to whether she had any earlier sexual experience, there was some indication that this was not her first encounter. Certainly, she understood the nature of her new relationship after the second date. If she was not yet ready for intercourse, a little caution may have seemed advisable to her. (Jones told the court that she had not actually been menstruating but had told Salle she was in order to put him off.) Although Jones claimed in court not to have known why Salle wished to get a room with her, this testimony seems unlikely. Her prior conversation with Mabel about getting money was explicit enough. What remained indisputable was the degree of autonomy exercised by Almary. She may not have understood everything she was getting into, but she certainly knew enough to lie to Salle about her age—and thus to guarantee that the enjoyably dangerous situation continued.

After Salle and Jones had intercourse, Mabel Springer came into their room and asked Almary if she had received any money from Salle. When told no, Mabel saw to it that John paid up. The court decided that this demonstrated Mabel to be the damning influence. As the judge commented: "I do not believe the boy would have done what he did had it not been for the influence of the married woman who lived in the same building where the girl lived . . . and she did not go until this married woman took her out into the toilet and said, 'Now Almary, Peter and I are going to a room, and Peter is going to give me ten dollars. I will make John give you five if you will go with him.' And finally the little girl said 'Yes,' she would go."[44] However, this interpretation was not supported by any testimony at the grand jury hearing. Jones herself testified only that Mabel told her that John Salle wanted to get a room with her. Jones provided no indication that she was coerced by Mabel Springer into doing anything.

It seems unlikely that either Almary Jones or Mabel Springer was coerced into an action against her moral code. To the contrary, both the married Mrs. Springer and the independent Miss Jones seem to have been fairly hell-bent on doing precisely what they wanted. Those wants included a few beers, some dancing, the picture show, and a little cash for a little sex with a couple of hard-working, respectable young fellows. Obtaining those rewards required the two women to do some negotiating with the young men, negotiations that had less to do with money than with the sex that might be available. Their agreements reflected both knowledge and a degree of accord between all parties as to what was appropriate and what could be had for what cost. None of the four challenged these fundamental understandings. It was not odd or "insulting," to use the language of the reformers, to the women that John and Pete had sexual designs on them. Almary and Mabel had their own scheme, and the men found this perfectly reasonable as well.

This mutuality of interest and purpose, a sensibility shared by all
four parties and by their numerous friends, testifies to the altered
sexual reality emerging at the beginning of the new century. Despite
the judge's attempts to paint Almary Jones as an innocent victim, few
of those involved agreed. Her eager participation in the relationship
with Salle may have made her character dubious to many, but for others it must have reinforced the emergence of a new code of acceptable conduct. Just as the popular vision (as mediated on screen and
stage) began to include female desire for the first time, private individuals—the first generation of young people impacted by and involved with the development of that vision—recognized women as
active and equal players in sexual affairs. Women such as Almary and
Mabel saw themselves as sexual actors in their own right; perhaps
even more significant, the young men shared that sensibility with
them. Negotiating a new sexual code did not necessarily entail an exchange of cash, although it certainly might.[45] What that negotiation
demanded was parity—a sense of, if not equal, at least equivalent desire by both men and women.

The testimony in the Salle case demonstrates well this symmetry.
However, the consternation and confusion surrounding the case
make it clear that this new public sexuality was as yet a language
under construction. Its syntax and grammar remained undesigned,
and its vocabulary still lay encoded in the conversations of the past.
The grand jury inquisition of Almary Jones was but one particularly
virulent reflection of the conflict between old and new. She received
little sympathy, despite the assault upon her honor that would send
John Salle to prison for five years.

By 1910, many members of the community understood that the
rationale for the law on statutory rape had been eroded by a new sexual ethic. Some jurors felt trapped into making judgments they could
not truly support. When another young man, Frank Silva, was convicted for a similar crime two years later, the jurors were beside
themselves with anger at being forced to punish what they truly did
not see as a crime. Four days after Silva's conviction for statutory
rape, his lawyers applied for probation, calling upon an unusual
source for support. In a remarkable document, the jurors themselves
pleaded for mercy for the man they had just convicted: "While we

firmly believe that we, as citizens and jurors, could do nothing under an oath except to render a verdict of guilty in view of the law and the evidence in said cause, we do believe that in view of the previous good character and habits of the defendant, and considering all the circumstances connected with said cause, that the minimum of five years in the penitentiary would be entirely out of proportion to the offense charged."[46]

The jury reacted with frustration to a case that indicated complicity between two young people. The indictment against Silva was brought nine months after the incident and coincided with the placement of the alleged victim, Florence Lewis, into a detention home for wayward girls. Such assignment was a common punishment levied against sexually active female teens. Lewis's presence there, as well as a doctor's testimony that examination revealed "her hymen was lacerated and the conditions showed that she had had sexual intercourse with some person,"[47] undoubtedly created suspicion in the minds of the jury as to the degree of victimization involved in this crime.

The testimony in the Silva case was actually much more conflicted than that in the Salle case. Lewis, under pressure at the detention home many months after the incident, claimed that Silva invited her to a Portuguese community picnic in Folsom, a nearby farm town, the previous May; his friend Bill escorted her friend Minnie. According to Lewis, somewhere along the way to the picnic, Silva demanded that she "come through or get out and walk."[48] Lewis testified that they crawled under some barbed wire into a field and had intercourse. When asked by the grand jury why she had consented, Lewis responded, "Well, I was afraid he was going to leave me there. I did not want to stay there. I did not know the road well enough to go home."[49] Although Lewis also expressed concern for her safety, claiming that Silva was "an awful mean-tempered man,"[50] the jury was apparently surprised that Lewis would surrender her virtue over what seemed like such a minor inconvenience.

The grand jury heard other testimony that cast doubt on Lewis's version of the affair. According to her friend Minnie, Lewis confided the next day that a proposition had been made on the way home from the picnic but that Silva "couldn't do anything."[51] Frank Silva denied his guilt to the end, although some of his friends testified against him. According to buddy Joseph Dias, Silva bragged later that both he and Bill had intercourse with Florence and "he stated he ruined her and put eight stitches in her."[52] Though no one else testified to a multiple rape and no such charges were brought, the phrase "eight stitches" caused some disquiet among the grand jurors. They asked Dias, "Did you understand him to say she had to be sewed up?" "Yes," he replied.[53] Yet when another friend, Luis Maria, testified to a similar conversation, a new meaning emerged. Maria recalled: "He said, 'I heard you were out with three girls.' I says, 'Yes.' He says, 'I give seven inches' or 'seven stitches.' I could not remember." Whether Silva said "inches" or "stitches" dominated the next few sections of the transcript. The court decided that Silva must have said "stitches" and queried Luis Maria. "What did he refer to when he mentioned seven stitches; what did he mean?" Responded the reluctant friend, "I guess he meant he 'fucked' the girl or something."[54]

As with John Salle two years earlier, numerous friends of the twenty-three-year-old Silva, a Southern Pacific laborer, testified to his good character. The combination of such testimony with Florence Lewis's "unladylike" conduct persuaded the jury that although a violation of the law may have occurred, justice had not been served. Officers of the court and the judge did not agree. According to probation officer M. J. Sullivan, Silva was guilty before any act of intercourse had taken place. In his report to the judge, an outraged Sullivan noted that Silva was "23 years of age and he admitted on the witness stand that he took this child of 14 years to a picnic, having known her only about a week. This in itself was reprehensible."[55]

The judge agreed and not only thundered his disapproval of the actions taken by Silva and Lewis but also proclaimed the beliefs of what was rapidly becoming a bygone era. Though acknowledging the testimony that Silva came from a fine family and was a faithful employee, the judge noted that Silva not only had had intercourse with Lewis but also had slept with another girl during the trial itself. "What hope would there be if I turned you loose in the community, that tomorrow you would not take another girl and treat her the same way?" queried the judge, not altogether unreasonably. Despite giving some rather contradictory advice ("If you want to have intercourse

with women, have it with women and not with babies"), the judge
made clear what the jury and so many members of the community
somehow failed to grasp: "Silva, in a country where girls are not pure,
men do not marry them and make good homes; in a country where
there are no good homes, there is no good government, because all
good government is builded upon the cornerstone of the good
homes; and in a country where there is no good government, there is
no security for life, property or liberty."[56] He went on: "By your assaulting the virtue of girls, . . . you were assaulting the very foundation of the cornerstone of the government; you are assaulting the very
principles upon which the happiness of the race depends."[57] Silva
was sentenced to seven years in prison, and the Constitution was
saved.

The judge in this case undoubtedly felt the need for such a clear
statement of principle precisely because he seemed so alone in its
maintenance. Silva was one of the last Sacramento men to serve time
for consensual sex with an underage woman. Indeed, his family's immigrant status, seemingly underplayed in all the testimony about his
respectability, may have been the factor that ultimately sent him to
prison at a time when such harsh sentences were on the wane.
Although Arthur Silkwood, accused of two such incidents and acquitted on one count, served a year in county jail in 1914,[58] probation had
become the rule by World War I. This consistent unwillingness to
punish or, at times, even to convict provides strong evidence of a dramatic shift in community values on the subject of sexual activity.

In the world described by the judge in the Silva case, the state had
replaced the church as the arbiter and protector of moral order. The
home and government collapsed into a single entity, replacing God's
universe, guarded so zealously by the church in an earlier time. It is
this imagery that we associate so directly with the sexual order that
preceded ours and with which we periodically find ourselves uncom-
fortably confronted. Yet early in the century that vision had begun to
break down dramatically throughout the country. For the first time
there was an open dialogue concerning the fact that mutual consent
governed most sexual activity and that such behavior lay outside the
purview of the criminal justice system. This recognition can be seen
in the solid community support afforded those accused of crimes in

such cases, the reluctance of juries to convict or recommend punishment, and eventually the decision by judges to suspend sentences for those who were convicted.[59]

III

By World War I, the Victorian assumptions about sexuality which dominated Progressive rhetoric were in tatters. Public imagery of women no longer conveyed purity and chastity. The movies and popular stage had made clear that women were deeply interested in expressions of erotic desire. Women on the screen initiated sexual contact, took responsibility for its development, and often enjoyed its pleasures without ill consequence. Not surprisingly, reformers roared that such films utterly lacked moral content. But, of course, the films did have a moral ethos—it simply differed from that of late-nineteenth-century middle-class culture.

In reconstructing public heterosexuality, the films reflected and helped build consensus for a vision of women as sexual beings. This consensus crossed class lines in the white community; though films depicted some sexually active women as disreputable or working-class, the overwhelming majority were represented, both by dress and lifestyle, as middle-class or, at least, upwardly mobile. Although the burlesque girl may have been the symbol of sexual precociousness, the middle-class wife or girlfriend demonstrated an equal degree of pleasure in expressing her desire.

It is important to grasp the visual power of this moment. As the first films made their way through the country and enthralled a national audience, they presented images of women that rang true with many in the audience. At precisely the moment that the Progressive ideologues launched their assault on prostitution, vice, and male lust, the films offered a counterdiscourse that manipulated prostitution, redefined vice, and contextualized lust as a two-party action. The audiences listening to both ideologies rejected the Progressives, whose vision of the world bore so little resemblance to their own, and welcomed the films as affirmation and agreeable entertainment.

In towns like Sacramento, these discourses redefined public heterosexuality. Increasingly, judges who defended womanhood and the family as understood by the Progressives found themselves voices in the wilderness. They railed alone in communities that cared deeply about their members. These were small towns in which many people knew each other, had grown up together, and worked together as adults. If the people of Sacramento had no desire to prosecute and convict statutory rape cases by 1910, it was not because they had fallen prey to a nameless, alienating society that promoted immoral character. On the contrary, it was because everyone's name was known. The Progressive rhetoric made no sense to the people of Sacramento. They knew the people accused of sexual crimes and knew dozens of others who behaved similarly but were never charged. They could not see evil in these actions; they and their neighbors engaged in these same activities and considered them harmless.

Indeed, the word "evil" had little meaning in this context anymore. The evil would have existed, as Salle's judge so eloquently commented, in the assault upon female virtue. Yet the testimony in these cases reveals that many women regarded virtue as a creature of their definition. They sculpted virtue to include sexual choice and the expression of desire. In doing so, they stood at odds with the moral authority of the community but in sync with popular culture. In this early configuration, we see a patterning for the social changes that would come to dominate the twentieth century.

The inclusion of desire into female identity, a central focus of the heterosexual vision, was not a triumphant process. The women discussed here did not wake up one morning and march through the streets, ushering in a world of sexual "liberation." In their contravention of community authority, these women and men were punished. As time went on, men were punished less by the courts, but women began to be punished more. Moral "delinquency" and moral "imbecility" emerged as terms to explain female sexual expression. Young women in particular found themselves sent to newly built detention homes and mental institutions. Sterilization was the fate awaiting thousands of women who ended up in such monuments to female protection offered by the Progressives.

Yet the rise of such institutions testifies to the depth of the changes being documented here. Early films, with their carefully etched promotion of female sexuality, and real-life women who insisted upon

expressing their own sexual desire, often at great cost, forced turn-of-
the-century society into a different realm of public sexuality. Even
those who did not approve of the films or the actions of these women
began to readjust their understanding of the heterosexual world
around them. This fundamental shift began before the popularization
of Freud and Krafft-Ebing, and it was not confined to major cities.
Well before the 1920s, in small communities as far removed from
New York as from the moon, both men and women had come to realize that sexual desire was not a gendered characteristic exclusive to
men nor a morally inappropriate trait in women. Heterosexual desire
became not only accepted but imperative. Its exercise and manage-
ment became a task for both women and men and the community at
large. The evidence from Sacramento and the early films testify to
the conflicts faced by all participants as the emerging sensibility and
the older codes wrestled for dominance in the arena of civic authority
and the popular imagination.

Chapter Three

The Twentieth-Century Way

Framing heterosexual desire in a public context involved more than simply providing positive and negative boundaries for heterosexual behavior. If the old maid resisted heterosexuality, she could be contained by ridicule; her social power could be thwarted through a celebration of female desire. However, this did not resolve a comparable problem—men who resisted the heterosexual imperative. In the emerging public sexual culture, such men needed to be marked and identified in a way that left no room for acceptability. To accomplish this, those promoting popular culture collapsed gender identity with sexual practice: what you did in bed determined who you were. If a man did not engage in heterosexual practice, he was not really male at all. Though this equation of maleness with heterosexuality might have appeared foolproof, in the end it created more problems than it resolved.

Female impersonator Julian Eltinge's artistry amazed early-twentieth-century vaudeville audiences. To listen to contemporary critics, one might suspect that no one had ever effected so successful an artifice as Eltinge's remarkable portrayal of the female form. Swirling in a cascade of color and movement, Eltinge was the very essence of femininity, singing and dancing in a variety of "international" presentations. A flushed 1909 *Variety* critic noted that in the "Incense Dance," with the "splendid setting, yellow predominating as the color," the impersonator "executes a dance while in feminine Oriental dress. His 'girl' is an artistic study, from the slippers to the coiffure."[1] Eltinge's popularity was legendary. After one performance the crowd went wild, refusing to leave for intermission until he had returned to the stage and spoken to them directly. Eltinge's artistry—the perfection of his mimicry—signaled to his audience that their most basic understandings of gender could be illusory.

Whereas Eltinge became increasingly celebrated, other men who dressed as women discovered a more sinister fame. Hounded by hired detectives, trapped in beachside comfort stations, members of the "queer" community in Long Beach, California, were forced into public view in 1914. These men often dressed in gorgeous female attire during grand private parties. The participants included some of the wealthiest and most respected residents of the resort town, located some thirty miles south of Los Angeles. The discovery of this thriving community brought up the same kinds of questions raised by the brilliant and beloved Eltinge. When the men of Long Beach dressed as women, they playfully disguised their gender but ultimately revealed something more threatening—their sexual practice.

I

The admiring fascination with public female impersonation, as embodied in Julian Eltinge, in the early twentieth century seems directly to contradict the furious witch-hunt pursued against those men who dressed similarly offstage in the privacy of their own homes and communities. However, this disjuncture is neither bizarre nor inexplicable. Instead the public obsession with gender deception on stage and the equally obsessive offstage crackdown are related phenomena that link questions of public gender presentation—how you tell a man from a woman—with more symbolic concerns. How did public gender presentation mark private sexual practice? What were the implications of "problematic" sexual practice for the cementing of gender definitions?

These concerns can be seen in the attempt to understand the gender "message" presented by impersonators such as Eltinge. Commentators expressed both fascination with impersonators and continuous surprise at their popularity. As critics and reviewers sought to understand the public's affection, they initiated a series of interrogations designed to interpret the gender stories being told by impersonators. Newspaper accounts detailed Eltinge's offstage activities in order to clarify the onstage gender confusion. Reporters sought out markers of gender that might make sense to audiences, might explain how a man who so brilliantly embodied femininity could actually still be a man. This curiosity reflects a plaintive desire for certainty at a time when such certainty had become increasingly elusive.

The interrogations into Eltinge's life highlighted social fears of unacceptable private sexual practice. Supportive investigators sought to demonstrate that the public sign of Eltinge's fame—his magnificent female portrayal—did not reflect a secret degeneracy. Eltinge, they insisted, was a "real man." However, his offstage equivalents—other men who dressed as women—were deemed "abominations"[2] lacking the finer "qualities of manhood."[3] Proper manhood was at stake here, and hidden sexual practice could determine it. Here was an answer to the gender confusion of the period. If one could identify a man's private sexual behaviors, one could then establish his gender identity with certainty. Sexual practice could be "read" through public presentation, and gender could be ascertained. Although some may have believed in a "third sex" in order to account for these strange behaviors, the critical need was to anchor the "first sex"—male.

Police in Long Beach faced a similar problem. They too sought to deduce sexual practice from public gender presentation and learned, to their dismay, that such determinations were not so easy. The hidden universe of sexual practice revealed in Long Beach demonstrated the instability of gender categories. People were not always who they seemed to be, and signs of "degeneracy" became increasingly diffuse. The discourse in Long Beach precisely echoed the vaudeville calls to certify manhood through the "sight" of hidden sexual practice, yet the realities in Long Beach reinforced the gender confusion witnessed in theaters across the country. The interrelationship of gender presentation and sexual practice asserted itself with particular ferocity at this moment. The discussions surrounding Eltinge and the documents from the Long Beach investigation make it clear that gender definition was deeply problematic at the turn of the century and that the connection between sexual practice and the nature of male and female occurred on the streets as well as on the stage.

Questions about the nature of male and female had already received serious attention in many parts of the country. Hastened by the pace of urbanization and the growing public presence of women, gender structures came under increasing challenge in the early twentieth century. As women began to clamor for civil rights and engaged in more visible and confrontational demonstrations during the Progressive Era, they forced a discussion of what constituted appropriate behavior for each gender. This discussion took place across a broad swath of American life and ranged from serious academic scholarship to witty ripostes in popular media. Earnest commentators expressed great fear that women had abandoned their proper tasks in the home in favor of social activism, whereas quipsters chortled about women in trousers who wanted to be men. Women themselves remained uncertain over the direction of their lives. Some argued that social reform was merely an extension of their role in the home, with the community but another wing of the household. Others demanded full political equality and seemed unconcerned that this might remove them from the shelter of femininity. Yet many women were concerned about traditional gender roles, and the fight for women's suffrage—the hot political topic of the era—was rife with controversy over whether the vote would strip women of those feminine qualities that made them different and special.

Gender-based political arguments affected men as well. They were forced to take sides and reevaluate traditional claims about gender roles. Moreover, gender reassessment was not limited to women; many thinkers scrutinized masculinity, too. Observers worried that the "softness" of modern life had stripped men of important male attributes. Weakened by technological convenience and cushioned by the niceties of middle-class culture, men had lost their essential toughness. Teddy Roosevelt, the "bully" president and inveterate cheerleader of this period, was particularly exasperated with what he saw as the decline of masculine vigor. He aggressively promoted "manly" pursuits such as hunting and boxing and exhorted men to return to proper masculine form.[4] This anxiety about the state of masculinity matched the concerns about femininity. Given the deep apprehension over gender, it is perhaps not surprising that a fascination with gender impersonation arose at this time; however, the attempt to sort out the confusion by linking sexual practice and gender seems an unexpected response to this widespread social anxiety.

That link is more commonly attributed to the determined efforts of *fin de siècle* sexologists such as Havelock Ellis, Richard von Krafft-Ebing, and Sigmund Freud, who are largely credited with the development of sexual pathology models based on observable "symptomatology" such as dress and behavior. Male and female homosexuals—the sexual inverts described by Krafft-Ebing and Ellis—exhibited their "disease" primarily through appearance or occupation signaling the "wrong" gender. However, the insights offered by the sexologists by themselves cannot explain the widespread and relatively rapid incorporation of the idea that a profound relationship existed between sexual behavior and gender identity. Much of the activity in the fierce struggle to resolve gender anxieties took place on the popular level. Such intense curiosity about gender permeates the popular culture of the period that we can only grant limited authority to the sexologists.[5]

II

The era from 1890 to World War I marked a heyday for entertainers who made their living impersonating members of the opposite sex.[6] Impersonators were among the most successful and highly paid stars during the first quarter of the twentieth century.[7] Although England had a music-hall tradition of drag comedy, female impersonation in the United States emerged from a different root—the immensely popular minstrel shows of the mid-nineteenth century. Characterized by hyperstylized, mocking portrayals of African Americans, minstrel shows provided many outside the South with their first and sometimes only imagery of blacks. Minstrel shows are remembered most for their caricatures of African American men, yet African American women were hardly immune. Some white men specialized in impersonating romantic female characters known as the "yaller girl."[8] Employing racist stereotypes of the "tragic mulatto," these portrayals often called for a more serious tone than ordinary minstrel fare and helped to train white female impersonators.[9] The minstrel show began to decline in the early twentieth century, and female impersonators moved into vaudeville. Many of the famed female impersonators of the period got their start on the minstrel-show circuit, playing black women, and their characterizations of white women drew forth interesting comparisons. As one critic noted, "Just as a white man makes the best stage Negro, so a man gives a more photographic interpretation of femininity than the average women is able to give."[10]

This extraordinary remark helps to explain some of the attraction provided by female impersonation. The "best stage Negro" was, by definition, an artificial production; the critic did not attempt to argue that white men made the best "real" Negroes. Similarly, femininity is regarded in this remark as performative—something best produced through thoughtful artifice by one who understands what the concept truly means.[11] This critic clearly believed female impersonation was a conversation between and among men, an art form designed by and for them. Additionally, because most photographic images were posed in this period, the critic's use of a photographic metaphor is telling. His support of "posed" femininity reinforces its element of performance—the fact that femininity is indeed "staged." That female impersonators could be said to offer a more authentic representation of femininity than could women themselves indicates the degree to which illusion and performance had become paramount in the struggle over gender.

Julian Eltinge's deceptive prowess made such comments possible. One of the premier vaudeville entertainers prior to World War I, Eltinge traveled extensively and attained enormous critical and financial success. His "perfect" replication of the female presence prompted awed responses from critics and audiences alike. Broadway's love affair with Eltinge began in 1905, and he joined the famed Cohan and Harris Minstrels for the 1908 season. When Eltinge reappeared as a solo act in 1909, *Variety* raved, "As an impersonator of girls, or 'the' impersonator of 'the' girl, Eltinge excels."[12] This "artist in female drawings"[13] created a stampede at the box office in 1910. Audiences poured into the vaudeville houses around the country to witness an artist said to be "as great a performer as there stands on the stage today."[14] On September 11, 1912, the Julian Eltinge Theater opened on Forty-second Street in New York to honor the wildly popular star.

Eltinge toured for many years with his comedy, "The Fascinating Widow," smashing attendance records everywhere.[15] The show spread his fame throughout the country and made him a very wealthy man.[16] Eltinge reigned as a prince of vaudeville from 1909 through the early twenties and even made several films.

Eltinge's primary rival, Bothwell Browne, also toured with the Cohan and Harris Minstrels, working primarily on the West Coast. Periodically he tried to break into big-time vaudeville, only to end up back on the road. Although he remained primarily a small-time, western phenomenon, Browne's celebrity as a regional figure was considerable and correctly reflected the national popularity of female impersonation.[17]

Eltinge and Browne were the most prominent of a large number of female impersonators who filled vaudeville houses around the country. Most of these acts ended up in small-time theaters, from stages on the outskirts of New York City to the swankier vaudeville houses in small- and medium-sized communities.[18] Throughout the country, newspaper accounts regularly discussed the most recent impersonation act, attesting to the broad popularity of this entertainment form. *Variety* seemed to believe that impersonators were more successful on the small-time circuit because theatergoers in the major urban areas believed themselves too sophisticated for the basic nature of most such routines. A performer would not make it in the big-time simply by dressing as a woman; one must display truly spectacular artistry. However, for "small time audiences not too highly educated in what is best in vaudeville sketches"[19] —in other words, virtually everyone outside the major New York City vaudeville halls— simple gender impersonation continued to hold fascination and delight, and audiences flocked to theaters to watch these entertainers display their talents. From the top to the bottom of the bill—from comedy to drama, from blackface to formal gowns—individuals breaking into vaudeville used female impersonation to pave their way. Some copied the established stylings of Eltinge or Browne, and others invented new routines, but most followed a well-established formula for how to present a female on stage, and their success was based on the authenticity of that imitation of life—not its creativity or originality.

One after another, they tried for fame and fell into obscurity. "[Grazer] makes up for his female impersonation well enough to deceive any one, even the wisest vaudeville habitué," commented *Variety* on one long-forgotten would-be Eltinge.[20] Sterling and Hutton proved less successful, fooling no one. They "open as a 'sister' act, but it is easily discerned that the larger of the two is male," noted the irritated reviewer. Even worse, the "man changes to a bathing suit doing the 'Gibson Girl' song used by Julian Eltinge years ago."[21] Better notices awaited a performer named Mary Elizabeth, who played the Diepenbeck Theater in Sacramento on the Orpheum circuit in October 1912. The reviewer for *Variety* delightedly reported that "Mary Elizabeth delivers a pleasing assortment of songs together with an amusing line of talk. The mystery that shrouds the identity of the singer gives added interest."[22] Two clever impersonators billed as "Love and Haight" also scored well with critics and audiences. *Variety* described their act: "[T]he shorter chap appears first in soubrettish attire and specializing in ballet dancing. The bigger fellow seems to have been paying close attention to Julian Eltinge." *Variety* felt "the boys should be able to get over in pop houses," thus relegating them to a lesser but nevertheless worthwhile circuit.[23] Francis Yates did "something a little different from other female impersonators in vaudeville," working as "both a girl and a man." Yates would "have to step some before he will reach the Eltinge or Bothwell Browne class," but his voice was "good, both in natural and falsetto tones."[24] A select few impersonators, including British star Malcolm Scott, graduated from vaudeville to Broadway. "Scott got over very big," primarily through his historical impersonations of Catherine Parr and Henry VIII, even though, as reviewers noted, "the subject is unfamiliar to vaudeville patrons." Having wowed them in the big city, Scott, it seemed, "could stand the top billing and get over almost anywhere."[25]

Impersonators relied upon a world that was familiar yet special to audiences. The reviewers assumed that audiences were fascinated by the performers' flamboyant clothing, occasionally mocking impersonation acts as glorified fashion shows seemingly aimed only at women. Such curmudgeonly attitudes were not uniformly shared, a fact evidenced both by full theaters and the less carping reviewers who gave detailed descriptions of the costumes. Whether noting Bothwell Browne's "beautiful black dress with a train . . . gorgeously trimmed with beads and ribbons"[26] or highlighting Julian Eltinge's "magnificent black gown" worn "draped from his right shoulder,"[27] these writers confirmed what some already suspected—that "no woman could have worn the dress to more perfect advantage."[28]

Impersonation seemed to offer men the opportunity to take power over representations of femininity. Eltinge could crystallize the essence of what it meant to be female into a few specific surface details. In principle, this simplification could be reassuring. Eltinge's characterizations offered to fix femininity at a straightforward and superficial level and reinforced male authority over that image. One critic snorted that "it takes a man after all to show women the path to beauty. Julian Eltinge has so developed female impersonation that today he is the glass of fashion for the thousands of women in search of beauty secrets."[29] The New York *Dramatic Mirror* marveled that Eltinge gave "great attention to the many details of apparel with which women are very familiar."[30] In the Midwest, an enterprising reporter for the *Cincinnati Times Star*, claiming to document "a few excerpts from conversations heard in the elongated line that awaited seat sale for the special matinee of Julian Eltinge," offered quotes from swooning young girls.[31] "I always love to see him because I think he is the loveliest girl," reported one with unconscious irony. To another, Eltinge was "the prettiest woman I ever saw." Two of the young admirers in line looked to Eltinge for guidance on enhancing their femininity. "I'm a modiste," admitted one. "I want to see him just to get a few new ideas on the latest gowns."[32] According to another Cincinnati reporter, "To the ladies . . . this female impersonator has become an idealized clothes horse. He takes the latest creations with which fashion would bedeck the female form and shows the opposite sex how they should be worn."[33] A wry reviewer for the *St. Louis Globe* clarified the ironies of female impersonation, chortling: "In these days of the feminism, when it is gradually dawning on many that 'mere man' is something more than 'mere man,' . . . sardonic fun can be extracted from the circumstances that another 'mere man,'

Julian Eltinge, is easily able to wear and disport himself in feminine togs in a manner that must cause the pangs of an entirely novel jealousy to rise in many a woman."[34]

This reporter may have wished to locate anxiety in female jealousy, but Eltinge's success provoked much greater concern elsewhere. What were men to make of the fact that Eltinge seemed so fascinated with the accoutrements of femininity? Eltinge continued his act after the curtain fell through *The Julian Eltinge Magazine*, published in 1912 and 1913. The magazine shared makeup and beauty secrets and emphasized his fashion know-how and appeal.[35] One 1912 press release trumpeted that "he has fans and combs, silk hosiery and French petticoats galore. His shoes are made to order and no society girl is more particular about her heels and the fit."[36] A man who flaunted his French petticoats and bragged that he was more particular about his heels than a society girl raised more gender questions than he answered.

These issues accelerated when male reviewers, emphasizing Eltinge's skill and demonstrating his appeal to men as well as women, raised a troubling possibility: men might find this figure sexually attractive. The *Cincinnati Times Star* reporter included a male echo to the comments from Eltinge's enthusiastic female cadre: "'I want to see him,' said a man, 'because I think he's the swellest dame that ever wore down the boards.'"[37] *Variety* attempted to maneuver through the difficulty with careful wording: "As a girl on the stage any man would rave over the genuine reproduction of Eltinge's impersonation. His 'Brinkley Girl' is a dream; his 'Bathing Girl' a gasp."[38]

By emphasizing that it was not Eltinge himself but his artistic creation that might become the subject of male fantasy, *Variety* revealed the anxieties that impersonation provoked. Though the subject of the outward discussion was femininity, the real issue was the nature of masculinity. If Eltinge could be an object of heterosexual male fantasy, was he really a man? "Mere man," as the St. Louis reporter sarcastically phrased it, had indeed become the issue, and male responses to female impersonation expressed great distress. The fascination with beautiful fashions and personal attractiveness can be read as both admiration and discomfort. The impersonators' beauty, as produced on stage, magnified not only their talents but also their capacity to undermine gender certainty.

Female impersonation was both deeply threatening and an extremely important signifier of what it meant to be an adult male, because female impersonators were, of course, actually men. The question of Eltinge's identity provoked significant disquiet, reflecting a need to determine a male gender that was not open to interpretation. This concern played itself out in obsessive discussions of how the star's private behavior and dress either replicated or contradicted his performing persona. This search produced multiple gender presentations—in their own way equally, and even more desperately, performative.

Julian Eltinge's maleness took many forms. Most photos of Eltinge, a notorious publicity hound, pointedly depicted him out of female attire. When he brought his hit play to Wisconsin, for example, the *Milwaukee Journal* juxtaposed a photo of an aggressive, forceful-looking Eltinge, cigar in outreached hand, against a picture of Eltinge as "The Fascinating Widow."[39] In other well-circulated publicity photos, images of his female characters interacted with the undisguised star. One montage showed Eltinge in shirtsleeves athletically rowing a boat that contained four of his female creations, who coyly enjoyed his vigorous masculinity.[40] The popular press tended to emphasize Eltinge's virility. He was "a good looking fellow on the street; well built and perhaps a little beyond the ordinary attractive man to an impressionable young woman," remarked *Variety*.[41] According to other reports, Eltinge was nothing less than a pugilistic marvel. "I seen him fight once in Pittsburgh and I'm for him," growled a male supporter in Cincinnati; others reportedly confused him with "Jim Flynn, the white hope," when the "husky built chap, broad of shoulder and likewise of girth" strolled by: "'That's him,' squealed a girl. 'You're crazy,' answered another. 'Why Eltinge is a little bit of a chap. That looks like a prize fighter.'"[42]

Eltinge worked tirelessly to promote an image of himself that reinforced traditional masculine norms. Virtually all publicity dealing with Eltinge (and reams were produced) highlighted his "manly" qualities. One early article, dating from his initial foray into impersonation, took the direct approach. "Julian Eltinge Isn't Effeminate

When He Gets His Corsets Off" ran the headline over a picture of Eltinge dressed in feminine garb. The story described Eltinge's refusing to accept flowers handed him over the footlights and requesting instead the results of the first race at Belmont.[43] The *Boston Traveler* reassured its theatergoing readers with a headline insisting: "Eltinge Really a Manly Chap, In Fact His Name Is Bill Dalton."[44] Male reporters brought in to watch Eltinge "become" a woman backstage always expressed some discomfort, which was ultimately alleviated by proper displays of gender. In Boston, reporter William Sage wrote of being overwhelmed by Eltinge's femininity as the impersonator dressed: "I presume I would have been flying down the street if Eltinge had not tipped over a tray of hairpins. The swear words that ripped so easily from his lips in a fine manly voice relieved us both. They soothed his anger and reassured me of his masculinity."[45]

Newspaper stories about Eltinge's private life offered further relief from gender anxiety. Eltinge claimed to be a farmer with a "working" farm on Long Island. "There he gets right down to things masculine and earthy. He is an ardent amateur farmer; he has a handy way about him too and likes to putter about doing odd jobs of painting and plumbing," reported the *Cincinnati Commercial*.[46] The *Toledo Blade* reminded audiences in Ohio that Eltinge "has been known to hold his own in a boxing bout with Jim Corbet, is a winner in a rowing match and has always been in the front rank of many sports dear to manly men." The writer felt more secure "knowing these things, as Mr. Eltinge has been careful that they should be known."[47]

Indeed, Julian Eltinge was very careful that such things should not only be known but widely advertised in advance of all his performances. No one matched Eltinge's own continuous output of information identifying himself as genuinely male. One press release revealed that "the fluffy skirt and dainty bodice hide the figure of an athlete and more than one officious person has been taught a thing or two in upper cuts and strong blows."[48] In interviews Eltinge often told reporters of his affection for male attire and masculine activity. "The dame stuff doesn't appeal to me. When I retire I hope to get into overalls and duck the barber."[49]

Star impersonators such as Eltinge needed to prove their masculinity and avoid allegations of effeminacy at all costs. This created problems for most, and their careers often rose or fell on their capacity to successfully negotiate this contested terrain, which was unstable and constantly shifting. Accusations of effeminacy did not merely apply to public activity; they also called into question the nature of private sexual behavior and its impact on the public's understanding of the individual's gender. Julian Eltinge and his compatriots in impersonation found themselves scrutinized not only for proof of a clearly readable and assignable gender but for secret signs of "degeneracy" as well.

Concern over the possibility of sexual perversion in gender impersonation arose early and often. In a 1906 interview Eltinge claimed to dislike female impersonation because "many of the impersonators have given the outsider good cause to believe all he hears of a man who wears women's clothes on stage." The soon-to-be star felt he could win over his colleagues, however. "It is not pleasant to go into a house on a Monday morning and be regarded with suspicion by my fellow players, but I find that they soon learn that I am a real man, and by Wednesday I have gained their respect."[50]

Eltinge's statement was quite typical of remarks that appeared in reviews and interviews. Asserting one's status as a "real man" seemed to address, in order to deny, the possibility of male homosexuality. Critics used such characterizations both to clarify Eltinge's special status and to reassure the public. *Variety* directed attention to Eltinge's "fine manly self"[51] even while praising his remarkable feminine characterizations. New York's *Dramatic Mirror* thought Eltinge "the manliest man" and "the girliest girl."[52] The *Boston Transcript* perhaps stated people's true feelings with its carefully worded praise that Eltinge was "unique in being able to look like a mannish man and a convincing woman at different times,"[53] thus casting probably quite appropriate doubt as to which constituted the greater performance.

Eltinge's sufferings over the aspersions heaped upon his manhood became the stuff of legend. When a stagehand aimed a "malignant grin" at Eltinge during a rehearsal in 1914, he was reported to have stopped work in order to inform one and all: "Now, I'm a man. I may be a female impersonator, but—the first guy that makes a crack about me is going to get a punch in the mush, do you get me?"[54] The report indicated that this was a typical occurrence for Eltinge, whom it quoted as complaining: "I'm a little sore. I have endured much. Things that you cannot punch a guy on the jaw for get my goat."[55] One reporter noted in 1912 that "like all outsiders, Eltinge didn't understand the contempt in which the man who plays a woman's part seriously is held by people off the stage" and quoted Eltinge in rueful response: "If I had known what they think, I would never have taken up the work seriously."[56] The author regaled his readers with stories of Eltinge's fights with sneering stagehands and critics, concluding that he enjoyed retelling such "fierce manly beserker things of Eltinge because he's too good a chap to be tarred with the stick that is applied with all propriety to the other fellows."[57]

The vehement dislike of female impersonators seems to have become more pronounced as their prominence increased. Though isolated barbs appeared prior to 1910, by 1913 virtually every article about Eltinge or his colleagues specifically addressed the potential "offensiveness" of the performer. "In spite of a well defined popular prejudice against female impersonators, the public seems to regard Eltinge as away from others in this class," noted the *Stage Pictorial* in 1913.[58] The *New York Evening World* offered an even more direct defense: "There are a host of female impersonators. And those who are not abominations are pests. Eltinge is the exception."[59]

Bothwell Browne's career difficulties make clear that the terms "manly" and "effeminate," officially descriptions of gender, were in fact codes for "deviant" sexuality. Browne could not escape being labeled as "offensive" because he forced questions of sexuality to the surface, drawing critical scorn in New York for being too "female." When Browne opened his disastrous show "Miss Jack," the critics found him loathsome. One reviewer called his characterization of a young schoolgirl "insipid and disgusting" and sneered that the "'gorgeous array of costumes' with which the impersonator arrayed himself . . . only added to the feeling of disgust for the entire performance."[60]

Many observers seemed particularly offended by the exaggerated effeminacy and erotic implications of Browne's work. One 1910 critic described Browne's specialty road act, the "Serpent Dance," as "a wiggling dance with nothing but gauze over the pit of his stomach."[61]

The *Los Angeles Examiner* offered the following, more detailed, description of the "Serpent of the Nile" from Browne's 1913 road tour: "Cleopatra, fondling the reptile, then holding it from her in horrible fascination of fear, determined upon death, yet putting it away from her, finally crushes the venomed head to her bosom and expires in ecstatic agony."[62] According to Browne's press releases, his snakes were live and dangerous, and one can imagine the impact upon the stunned audience of seeing a writhing "venomed head" and an impersonator collapsed on stage in "ecstatic agony." It is no wonder that Browne emerged as such a controversial figure; he went further than Eltinge and deployed specifically erotic imagery intended to provoke his audience sexually. The *Examiner* reviewer expressed genuine discomfort, noting that the performance was "not less suggestive by reason of the sex of the performer."[63] This suggestive quality seems to have been an underlying issue whenever Browne or Eltinge took the stage. Reviewers' comments reflected a concern that male audiences might be aroused by the impersonator and that the performer hoped for just such a result.

The accusations of sexual deviancy that tarred Bothwell Browne also dogged Julian Eltinge, despite the latter's greater fame. A remarkable 1913 article by entertainment writer Amy Leslie that appeared in the *Detroit News*, reprinted in its entirety from the *Chicago Daily News*, clarified Eltinge's dilemma. Leslie noted that Eltinge, "brawny, intensely masculine and carrying well his own name of Bill Dalton, has the objectionable and difficult field of female impersonation all to himself, because the age loathes the usual creeping male defective who warbles soprano and decks himself in the frocks and frills of womankind." She excoriated commercial managers who had "swept Broadway of all its lisping gentlemen who walked from the waist up . . . and put the delicatessen undesirables within reach of a paint and powder box and substituted them for a chorus."[64] The writer wanted to make sure that her readers understood exactly the subject of her assault, and she offered enough descriptive detail that there could be no mistake. Though acknowledging that in earlier times and in other cultures there were places for effeminate men, Leslie raged that "these freaks disporting themselves clammily before rather irritated audiences have nothing in

common with talent . . . and are a flaming insult to any intelligent, nor-
mally healthy and sane audience." She described them as "writhing,
playing with time and fate, ignoring mind and morals and going
about with hideous painted lips and extravagant clothes. . . . They are
nearly always full of irresponsible gayety and much quiet wit of the
frivolous empty sort . . . their atmosphere is fetid and dank, cryptic or
[*sic*] meaning and abominable." She pitied Eltinge, who was "brawl-
ing and stampeding out his fury half the time because these creatures
who always flock together are 'crazy about him.'"[65] The article closed
with the scandalous tale of a night when these "pariahs with the
wristwatch" bribed a guard into letting them meet Eltinge at the
stage door. "Eltinge stepped out, caught sight of their fanciful ensem-
ble, and let out a roar out of him that shook the scenery. His pretty
wig was off, his black jet sleeves rolled up to fight, and he looked like
a stricken bull in the arena. The prim gentles fled. One of them
yelled, 'Somebody throw her a fish; she's a sea lion.'"[66]

Leslie's rage was clearly marked and precisely aimed at the male
homosexual subculture circling the entertainment industry in major
urban areas. She used numerous allusions to homosexuality that were
already in common usage or would shortly enter the lexicon. Perhaps
the most telling information is the marvelous story at the end, revealing a "camp" sensibility among the "prim gentles" who refer to
Eltinge with a sisterly "she." Obviously, the men running from the
roaring Eltinge saw him as one of their own.

Leslie's article reveals the connection between the subtext present
in discussions of how the impersonator performed his gender both on
and off stage and the real issues of sexuality at stake.[67] In their ongoing fascination with how Eltinge and others either avoided or fell into
the "trap" of effeminacy, critics demonstrated anxiety over sexual
practice and its relationship to an anchored, visible, and imperme-
able notion of masculinity. "Male defectives" may have "decked
themselves in the frocks and frills of womankind," but surely they
could be differentiated from the "brawny, intensely masculine" female impersonator Julian Eltinge. Manliness may have been the
term, but sexual perversity was the issue. The two came together in
critical discussions of Eltinge and other impersonators.

As reviewers probed this question, they situated themselves within a debate taking place in communities around the country. Newspaper and court records from towns far from New York (or Detroit and Chicago) indicate that homosexuality was not only well known but also the subject of precisely the kind of controversy present in the rhetoric surrounding impersonators. Police activity in various parts of the country inadvertently alerted residents to a pre-Kinseyan recognition: homosexual activity was widespread. Proclaiming an assault on the vice that had somehow escaped the city, police and prosecutors sought out male "perverts," only to discover that their prey remained indistinguishable from themselves. It was a confusion familiar to those who witnessed impersonation on stage, fearing but unable to be sure of what lay hidden under the beautiful costumes. In the real world, unprotected by the reassuring fall of the final curtain, the chaos played itself out with even greater uncertainty than on the entertainment stage—and for much higher stakes.

III

Sacramento courts occasionally prosecuted "crimes against nature," producing a widely varied set of judgments. In an 1898 trial, an individual who gave his name as Ah Fook was charged with "assault with intent to commit the infamous crime against nature, to wit sodomy," only to be acquitted when his lawyer persuaded the jury that Elwood Theobald, the complaining witness, had consented to the act.[68] In a particularly fascinating case, three men were arrested together in July 1905 for "infamous crimes against nature." George Roehmer was the complaining witness against William Mitchell, Frank DeFrank, and John Kagee. Mitchell went on trial first, in October 1905. When the defense attempted to get a jury instruction pointing to Roehmer's willing involvement, the judge refused, telling the jury that although the victim had not resisted the act, "the law resists for him." The jury was out only twenty minutes before they returned with a guilty verdict. William Mitchell received fifteen years in prison.

John Kagee stood trial next, with far different results. The *Sacramento Bee* pointed to the testimony on his behalf from his "wonderful mother," but Kagee's real advantage over Mitchell was having a much better lawyer. Although the judge again insisted that Roehmer's consent was immaterial, the defense attorney requested, and won, a particular instruction that helped members of the jury do what some clearly wanted to do—rescue a local fellow from jail. The judge ordered that if the jury believed "from the evidence that the prosecuting witness aided, assisted, and abetted the act charged, then he became an accomplice," and "a conviction cannot be had on the testimony of an accomplice." It was a brilliant strategy, and the jury deadlocked; Kagee was released. Five days later, the charges against DeFrank were dropped.[69]

Sacramento residents lived with the knowledge that members of their community engaged in homosexual conduct. In 1906 and 1907, the *Sacramento Bee* reported on a group of homosexual men known to gather at the livery stable.[70] Following the arrest of a popular local pugilist, the paper also warned that boxers engaging in homosexuality often frequented a particular section of the Sacramento River.[71] Tolerance for such behavior depended in large part upon the strength of one's local ties. Harry Collins, a forty-five-year-old visitor to Sacramento accused of having sodomy with a Sacramento man in 1907, received little sympathy (despite his fainting in the court); he was convicted and sentenced to twenty-five years in San Quentin.[72] Yet twenty-year-old William Donovan, also tried in 1907, had his mother and various friends testify in his behalf and received an un-heard-of suspended sentence. In fact, he was treated as a juvenile and placed under the supervision of probation officer Dan Healy.[73]

The recurring thread in these varied responses was a recognition that the accused men might genuinely belong to the community. The "criminality" of their behavior seemed to hinge upon whether they were town folks. As a result, juries did not universally condemn homosexual behavior but instead looked at each specific case and based judgment on the degree of consent and whether the accused was "one of them." The people in Sacramento understood that homosexual practice existed in their community and recognized their neighbors as participants. In the first few years of this century, this kind of knowledge seems to have been received quietly and with no visible panic. Yet as time passed and the struggle over gender definition became more pronounced, homosexuality began to occupy a more contested site in the public arena.

After fifty men in Long Beach, California, were arrested as social vagrants in November 1914,[74] C. V. McClatchy, the powerful publisher of the *Sacramento Bee* and a noted scandalmonger, sent an undercover reporter to get the inside scoop. Expressing outrage that some defended these individuals against "character assassins," McClatchy took a nasty swipe at Progressive reformers who focused on prostitution but ignored homosexuality, howling that "common sense cannot conceive how intelligent people who would lash the Hagars of modern society from city to city . . . could ask the sanctuary of silence for men who would have defiled Sodom and Gomorrah."[75] McClatchy sent reporter Eugene Fisher to Long Beach as an undercover operative. Fisher dug up extensive and explicit information about the Long Beach vice squad's attack against male homosexuals. He also provided remarkably detailed reports on sexual practice. His investigations revealed a large community of self-identified homosexuals, both male and female, based in Long Beach and extending throughout the Los Angeles area. Homosexuals from throughout the state gravitated there, indicating that a relatively wide communications network may have existed among California homosexuals.[76] Fisher's reports provided fascinating insights into this community and revealed the complexity of the heterosexual response. Before the story had wound to a close, the connections between gender and sexual practice would be drawn sharply as Long Beach authorities and juries searched in vain for a way to distinguish the guilty from the innocent.

Fisher's prime source, a young man named L. L. Rollins, had himself been arrested. Rollins offered a wealth of tales about a robust, complex homosexual community that saw itself as quintessentially modern and progressive and had its own culture and institutions. The world he described strongly resembled that of the "pariahs with the wrist watch" who flocked together and were "just crazy" for Eltinge—an important similarity, and one that is not coincidental.

The "society of queers" who held their "drags" at sites known as "96 clubs"[77] were among 2,000 to 5,000 homosexuals in the Los Angeles area in 1914.[78] Rollins claimed to know 200 "queers" personally,[79] including long-standing couples. In addition to the "96 clubs," parties generally took place in scattered private homes throughout the area. McClatchy obsessively demanded details, and Fisher obliged. He wrote up the gossip on an apparently famous party given by two Venice millionaires who had lived together for some years. According to Rollins's account, "about thirty prominent young men" had attended. "Each guest, when welcomed at the door, was given a silk kimono, wig and pair of slippers." An orgy of "unnatural practices" followed.[80] Rollins told of another party that had taken place only a few nights before his arrest. Fisher related that "fourteen young men were invited . . . with the premise that they would have the opportunity of meeting some of the prominent 'queers,' . . . and the further attraction that some 'chickens' as the new recruits in the vice are called, would be available."[81] The party continued in unprintable fashion for the *Bee*'s family newspaper. The guests "were served an elegant repast. . . . Instead of placecards, at each place was a candy representation of a man's private which was sucked and enjoyed by each guest to the evident amusement of all."[82] Rollins concluded with the information that "one or two of the young men were clad in women's clothing and entertained the gathering with music and song."[83]

Fisher acknowledged the widespread nature of these activities. He commented in an aside to his boss that "almost every man or boy seems to have encountered it in some phase or other during his life."[84] The reporter snarled that boys and girls were now at risk nationwide from "a form of vice that is more insidious in its operation, more diabolical in its effect and more degrading withal than any that hitherto have engaged the attention of delinquent and depraved men and women. It has now fastened its roots in these United States and threatens to sap the very lifeblood of society."[85] Though such hyperbole smacks of traditional Progressive flamboyance, Fisher clearly believed that homosexuality was widespread and entrenched. Like the contemporary sexologists with whom he had familiarized himself, Fisher found that "once used for this immoral purpose, boys and girls also are said to like the sensation and readily fall for it the second, third, and fourth times."[86]

Fisher and the police made an important distinction between the "sensation" so pleasurably discovered by threatened American youth and the gender of those with whom they shared that experience. The individuals arrested were charged with social vagrancy, not sodomy or crimes against nature. Both of the latter charges specifically identified male-to-male sexual activity that involved anal penetration. No laws existed in California to address the behavior testified to by these men.[87] Fisher's matter-of-fact tone in noting that the men were guilty of "nothing more nor less than 'cocksucking'"[88] belied his fury. The offensiveness of oral sex in and of itself seemed almost to rival that of the homosexual nature of the act.

"Historically, this is not a new form of vice," Fisher explained to McClatchy, referencing "the royalty and nobility of France, Italy, and other European countries in the time of Marie Antoinette."[89] Pointing out that "homosexualism" was a parallel but apparently not identical sexual practice, Fisher wrote: "It resembles homosexualism in the respect that men find their sexual pleasure and gratification with men and boys rather than women and women on the other hand are attracted sexually toward girls and women instead of the opposite sex."[90] Recalling Oscar Wilde's trial, Fisher reminded McClatchy of the "group of so called literary men and artists" engaged in "the practice of sodomy" and went on to clarify that "these creatures . . . are not even satisfied with this unnatural and degrading practice. . . . Their passion and desire still is for young boys and girls but they take their pleasure in the still more loathsome and disgusting way of applying their mouths to the private parts of their companions in crime."[91]

In his numerous reports, Fisher described incidents of oral sex extensively. Fellatio emerged as the focus of both police action and his own investigation. Although the homosexuality of the participants was not irrelevant, the practice of oral sex was absolutely crucial to the sense of moral crisis that surrounded the Long Beach case. One defendant who, the reporter sneered, had the temerity to go to court rather than kill himself, was "said to have practiced the infamy for more than nine years, being one who will 'go down' on another or will himself willingly and gladly submit to the outrage."[92] Fisher quoted Rollins as saying: "I have seen men . . . at a function of that kind . . . go around on their knees to various other persons present and attempt to 'go down' on them right before the crowd and seemingly they have no shame about it."[93] Further clarifying the separation between "homosexualism" and the practice under discussion, Fisher cited a local attorney who specialized in defending social vagrants. This gentleman verified that oral sex was a "vice as old as sodomy . . . practiced by both men and women for centuries."[94]

Although those engaged in oral sex seemed, according to Fisher's information, to be well aware of its timeless quality, they identified this sexual practice with a pet name that must have horrified Fisher and his police friends: the "twentieth-century way."[95] With this intonation, homosexuals—or "queers" as they called themselves—firmly and knowingly associated themselves with visions of progress and affirmative good. Americans saw the new century as the apotheosis of modernity and national ascendancy. The twentieth century offered the promise of great things: new technologies, a rising standard of living, and a vision of a glorious tomorrow. To incorporate a marginalized sexual practice into this vision of positive modernity demonstrated a remarkably self-conscious use of language. Whether they spoke with a sense of camp irony or merely to display boastful wit, the individuals using this phrase clearly saw themselves as a connected community tied by forms of sexual practice that they viewed as the wave of the future. "The twentieth-century way" reinforces our understanding of the complex homosexual subcultures that flourished not just in major cities but outside urban America as well.[96]

Perhaps out of fear that the name was too apt, authorities prosecuted those accused of practicing the "twentieth-century way" with a new vigor. In Long Beach, two men hired themselves out with the specific purpose of trapping and catching men engaged in oral sex with one another. According to Fisher, detectives B. C. Brown and W. H. Warren made the hunt a personal mission, taking their crusade around the country. Fisher claimed that the two came from Chicago, where Brown had worked for a private detective agency and Warren for the *Chicago Star* in a promotional capacity. On salary in Los Angeles, they requested and received permission to carry regular police badges.

Members of the Long Beach police commission originally scoffed at the possibility that such a vice existed in their town. The police agreed to pay Brown and Warren only if they could produce results, offering ten dollars per conviction. This arrangement undoubtedly contributed to the high number of arrests in this relatively small community.[97] The two detectives prowled public parks and restrooms searching for potential transgressors. According to the information given Fisher, most men were caught at the comfort station of the Long Beach Bathhouse. Fisher described in detail the tactics used by the detectives:

They would watch until they saw a man whom they thought to be given to this sort of thing and would attract his attention by putting their fingers through a hole in the board partition dividing the toilet walls. Upon looking through he would see a man's mouth close to the aperture and if were [sic] that kind of man and the suspicions of the officers correct, would stick his penis through the hole, whereupon the officers would stamp in some way, sometimes with indelible pencil and frequently with marker, and then rush in upon him.[98]

Warren and Brown's enterprise may have netted some positive publicity, yet it raised troubling questions as well. Fisher noted that one particular targeted individual had been "arrested while attempting to go down on Officer Warren."[99] This description of Warren as an active participant offers evidence that the two detectives engaged in entrapping sexual relations at least some of the time. This was a likely outcome given the context of the trap set by the detectives but, obviously, a more troubling one when the public attempted to assess whether Warren and Brown were "on the square," as the local police phrased it.[100]

The question reflected the problem faced both by those enjoying female impersonation on stage and those attempting to determine gender in the world around them. Visible cues, so important in the production of gender knowledge, were undermined by the emerging belief that the veiled universe of sexual practice could be just as determinant. When Warren and Brown sat waiting in a Long Beach comfort station, how did they determine that a man would be "given to this sort of thing"? How were the Southern California police, appropriately suspicious of two traveling detectives, to know if they were "on the square"?

It was exactly this problem that forced the acquittal of Herbert Lowe, a Long Beach defendant who brazenly demanded a trial. Even though five witnesses testified to his guilt and four claimed to have heard him confess, the jury refused to convict Lowe of social vagrancy. Attacking Brown and Warren, Lowe's attorney played upon precisely the same fears that had led to their hiring in the first place: "You don't know these stool pigeons who came here to 'get' our citizens; you do know Lowe. We don't need strangers to come here to ferret out crime." The defense attorney raged that "the hands of Special Officers Brown and Warren dripped with the blood of John Lamb," a Long Beach druggist who had committed suicide after being linked in print to the homosexual community. News accounts told how the clever attorney got to the heart of the matter. "'Look at this man who asks you to believe his testimony,' he said, pointing to Warren. 'See the puffs beneath the eyes, the sallow complexion, the sleek combed and oiled hair, the pink manicured finger nails—there is the degenerate.'"[101]

The telltale "signs" of degeneracy presented a fundamental obstacle. Everyone was suspect, and each had a list of traits by which to identify those who would engage in unmanly sexual practices. Just as theatrical audiences struggled to identify the gender of the impersonator on stage, so, too, did members of the community search for some definition by which to mark the face of perversity. Lowe's attorney pointed to effeminacy, demonstrated by pink manicures, and ill health, as seen in a sallow complexion and puffy eyes. Just as erotic femininity marked Bothwell Browne as offensive on stage and robust physicality identified Eltinge as "manly" off stage, this particular attorney demanded that fixed gender traits be applied in the community at large.

It was precisely the failure to find a comprehensive set of identifying characteristics that underscored the crisis in Long Beach. A smart attorney may have turned the tide for Lowe, but other homosexuals found themselves suddenly exposed, and their heterosexual neighbors expressed shock at the presence of such an unmarked vice.

Fisher noted with some concern that many of those in attendance at raided parties included "some of the wealthy and prominent men of the city, politicians, prominent business men, and even prominent churchmen."[102] Fisher contended that suicide in the face of such accusations demonstrated proof of appropriate masculinity, but even those who agreed with him must have found cold comfort in such verification. Commenting upon Long Beach druggist Lamb's death, the reporter declared that he "must still have some manhood and decency"; by contrast, "the degenerate, as a finished product, I understand, is utterly wanting in any of the finer qualities of manhood."[103] Manhood and degeneracy were completely incompatible. Suicide might be considered solid evidence of manhood, but it hardly constituted a workable means of gender identification.

Herbert Lowe's defense attorney turned the fear of the secret outsider onto the two detectives, actual strangers in the community. He could do so by playing upon the notion that hidden degeneracy remained fundamentally mysterious. A simple check of the prominent names on the arrest list reinforced that fact for the members of Lowe's jury and, despite their not-guilty verdict, undoubtedly intensified their sense of anxiety. If maleness as coded in public presentation could be undermined by transgressive sexual practice, how could gender be finally ascertained? If a private act could render one no longer truly male, it was essential that the act be known. The citizens of Long Beach looked for evidence of this pivotal hidden moment—a mark upon the body that could testify to the transgression. Yet, as the Long Beach investigation exemplified, such marks could not in fact be anchored to any certainties at all.

The private details unearthed in the Long Beach scandal provided images remarkably familiar to theatergoers across the country. The prominent men in Long Beach wore female finery that would have turned Julian Eltinge green with envy. One man, boasting "one of the finest wardrobes among the 'queer' people,"[104] carried a photograph of himself dressed in a gorgeous frock and a plumed hat sniffing flowers in front of his bungalow.[105] From the Venice partygoers who wore silk kimonos to the Southern California sheriff's son caught with a group of friends "undressed, and all . . . painted and powered [sic],"[106] male homosexuals celebrated their pleasure in "drag" attire that mimicked female form. The offense lay not so much in the trappings of female presentation as in the form of sexual practice such trappings represented. When the authorities looked at silk kimonos, they saw the twentieth-century way.

IV

The depth of the new concern can be seen in profoundly complicated images that ran simultaneously in turn-of-the-century America. In the same historical window, we find Julian Eltinge at the height of his career and police raiding the homes of men who "call each other by endearing names and dress in women's clothing at their balls and parties."[107] We see theaters filled with awed audiences swept up in the illusion of gender impersonation and roving detectives lurking in the shadows, hoping to trap those men whose sexual practices underscored the inability to identify gender with certitude. These are not oppositional images but pieces of the same puzzle.

Oral sex and homosexuality, separate but aligned symbols, became the focus of serious concern precisely because they could not be seen and therefore could not be known for certain. Seeing them had become essential to verifying gender, but this "simple" act proved virtually impossible. Absolute proof was elusive and came to be replaced by competing signs. Anyone could offer up a visible "mark" by which a person's sexual activity—and, hence, true gender—could be ascertained, and many did so. Herbert Lowe's attorney could secure an acquittal by calling detective Warren's "sallow complexion" to the jury's attention; theater critic Amy Leslie could point with equal ferocity to "lisping gentlemen full of irresponsible gayety" in order to defend Julian Eltinge. Who could privilege which sign? And how was anyone to know for certain?

The echoes of this struggle reverberated back and forth between the Long Beach courtroom and the vaudeville stage. The highly public debate over Eltinge and his colleagues helped verify the relationship between sexual practice and gender definition. Commentators in the popular press sought out the marks of "degenerate" sexual activity that could distinguish the "warbling male defective" from the "mannish" Julian Eltinge. Indeed, female impersonation on stage may have aided the process of developing codes by which to identify secret signs of gender dislocation. Such widespread discussion in newspapers around the country may well have helped produce a common language for sexual practice and gender identity. Certainly the obsessive concern with properly coding and categorizing such entertainers as Eltinge and Browne paralleled Long Beach residents' tormented attempts to decide which neighbors still retained the qualities of manhood and which utterly lacked in them. These anxieties may have played themselves out more safely under the protection of illusions that danced in the footlights, but even in that setting the fears that drove them remained.

The great irony, of course, is that the attempt to define gender and sexual practice in a way that reinforced appropriate public heterosexuality only made the situation more precarious. Visual cues that supposedly marked sexual practice were open to constant reassessment and individual interpretation, disturbing reminders that gender could not ever be known with certainty. Far from producing reassurance in a troubled era, the ongoing argument over sexual practice and gender definition produced continuous disruption and eternal instability. Instead of driving homosexuality from the public arena, this effort not only created an incontrovertible space for it but also made possible endless speculation on the best way to find it. In the end, despite all efforts to the contrary, the public sexual culture expanded to include both heterosexuality and its discontents.

Chapter Four

Why Mr. Nation
Wants a Divorce

In 1901, Edison released the comedy "Why Mr. Nation Wants a Divorce,"[1] which boldly satirized the impact of female social reform activities on the properly gendered household. In the film, a man taking care of an infant—a problematic premise to begin with—spanks the child when he tries to get out of bed. Afterward he gives the child a bottle of milk while reaching under the blanket to get a bottle of alcohol for himself. When his wife, dressed in a formidable black dress and imposing black bonnet, returns home to find her husband drinking the alcohol, she pulls him over her knee and spanks him.

In its attempt to elicit viewer sympathy for Mr. Nation, the film unintentionally pointed to a disturbing gap between its story and the audience's experience. This satire attacked on several fronts at once, assaulting not only famed temperance reformer Carrie Nation but also Prohibition as a cause, women who deserted their children for social housekeeping activities, and men who permitted themselves to be "infantilized" by their wives' behavior. Yet "Why Mr. Nation Wants a Divorce" pointed the viewer toward an unintended revelation. The film may have found divorce to be the answer for a nation of men faced by uppity women, but the film lied. Perhaps Mr. Nation did want a divorce, but overwhelmingly it was Mrs. Nation who filed the papers.

I

Those attempting to navigate the straits of singledom, confused by new rules and emerging redefinitions, may have believed they would find refuge in the safe and staid institution of marriage. If so, they were in for a rude awakening. The confusion inherent in the construction of a public heterosexuality now dominating relations among the unmarried had entered the world of marital relations as well. Those looking for asylum in the bonds of matrimony found only extensions of their own previous quandaries.

In the twentieth century, marriage completed its transformation from a very public institution representing church- and state-sanctioned social order to a private contract based upon highly personal needs. The goals and imperatives of marriage became less tied to the society at large and more specific to the two people who married. Though this trend culminated in the twentieth century, it had roots in earlier developments. The privatization of marriage grew as a result of economic changes that accelerated the separation of reproduction from sexuality. Birth rates declined throughout the nineteenth century as couples deliberately sought to limit the number of children they had and thereby to enhance family income in the newly industrializing world.[2] These choices indicate both a heightened level of discourse on sexual activity within marriage in the nineteenth century and a shift in focus. As couples planned their families, they forced the issues of personal desire and sexual need into the marital equation. Sexual duty, a long-standing marital command, ceased to hold its earlier value. The woman's "obligation" to engage in sexual relations in order to bear children made little sense in a situation where a limited number of children was sought. Both parties began to acknowledge that sex and reproduction needed to be seen separately.

As a result of this recognition, sexuality in marriage emerged as a focus of attention. Marital partners mapping this terrain placed increasing importance upon sexual desire and practice. After World War I and the emergence of a professionalized psychological discourse, this concern centered on the development of a personally satisfying sex life contained within marriage. Yet men and women struggled with these issues well before the war. Without any guidance from a new professional class, couples at the turn of the century developed new understandings that helped them negotiate the maze of modernized marital sexuality.

Documents from divorce cases provide important markers of the changing relations in marriage. Around the country, husbands and wives came into increasing conflict over their personal definitions of marriage. Surprisingly often, court testimony revealed these conflicts to be sexually based. Deeply gender-based assumptions about appropriate sexual behavior and its connection to cruelty appear in these records and help illustrate the issues at stake. Reading divorce records in order to identify normative marital behavior is a strategy to be used with caution, but this kind of testimony still remains one of the most vibrant sources available.

Marriage has always been a particularly rich subject for popular entertainment and social commentary, but the content of that wit and wisdom has changed with the times. The particular vision that emerged in the early twentieth century, though not dissimilar from earlier renderings, now lay directly counter to the experiences of many people, thus throwing the disjuncture between popular entertainment and "real life" into stark relief. That disjuncture is quite telling in this instance, and what it tells us is that heterosexual practice in marriage had become deeply troubled.

II

Using extremely traditional stereotypes of marital relations, popular artists began assaulting marriage for its perceived asexuality. Satirists ripped open the notion of marriage as the containment of sexuality within a controlled environment, portraying it instead as a sexually pointless relationship. Early films and vaudeville denounced marriage as an institution bereft of any sexual component. Popular representations of sexuality subverted middle-class rhetoric that celebrated marriage by utilizing jokes that were stunningly devoid of sexual creativity. In an age where filmmakers and performers seemed to compete over who could violate the largest number of sexual taboos, the incorporation of sexual pleasure into marital definition, so pronounced a controversy in the "real" world, was conspicuously absent from stage and screen. The onscreen images denied marriage's sexual possibilities at precisely the moment that aspect began to be emphasized off screen.

Filmmakers critiqued asexuality in marriage and placed the blame on women. In the movies, at least, married men and women did not engage in sexual activity. Wives became the great villains of humanity, sexless creatures who denied their husbands any opportunity to express and satisfy desire. This attack depicted male sexuality as a positive good straining against institutional restraints imposed by "the wife." Filmmakers located sexuality as a solely male prerogative and refused to portray desire anywhere within the marriage itself. Sexual activity among the married remained rooted in the image of the straying husband.

This representation of the asexual wife is particularly interesting given the rich set of contrasting cultural images that otherwise celebrated female sexuality. In a period filled with representations of sexually active women, marriage seemed to be the only site where sexual expression by a woman was presented as inconceivable. Films further emphasized this idea through portrayals of the asexual wife's common counterpart—the adulterous woman. Her sexual aggressiveness, the usual reason for her violation of the marriage vow, was inevitably punished by murder or suicide or sobbingly repented of in the arms of a boring but noble husband. Though such imagery may seem standard in our historical imagination for this period, it was in fact highly unusual for this kind of entertainment, flying in the face of both the dominant sexual imagery and the loud social conversation on marriage and sexual relations.

This somewhat surprising disjuncture is best illustrated by the fact that films about marriage inverted the "problem" to show, incorrectly, that it was men who wished to escape. Outside the theater, women initiated the vast majority of divorce suits; in them, they complained openly about all forms of male failure, including sexual performance. In the films, of course, men were always the dissatisfied party. These films distorted the marital issues of the day to privilege a particular form of male victimization. Indeed, many men may have felt victimized by the growing female exodus from marital confines. Movie conventions that reified patriarchy offered surprisingly potent counterrepresentations by which to combat women's assault on male power. No one could have known that the images presented would prove to be such a dramatically powerful tool by which to rewrite reality; the fact that it was predominantly women, not men, who fled from marriage when given the chance disappeared from history until only quite recently.

Filmmakers depicted marriage most commonly through stereotypical images of the henpecked husband and the overbearing wife. These icons functioned at several levels, beginning with critiques of female aggressive behavior and male impotence. In film and stage routines, this dynamic became the dominant representation of marital relations and reinforced the idea that marriage symbolized the antithesis of sexual possibility. Husbands and wives in popular entertainment were highly reminiscent of (respectively) the feminized male and the old maid, embodiments of asexuality and impotence.

Critics considered these archetypes hackneyed by 1910. *Variety* panned the vaudeville skit "Cupid at Home," playing at the Fifth Avenue Theatre in New York, for its passé premise: a wife attends club meetings, leaving her docile husband at home. The reviewer dryly noted that "they tell stories of how it knocked 'em off in '49" and scathingly insisted that "the one thing that will hold Cupid at Home back is the idea. It is not for the 20th century. And most of Monday night audience at the 5th Ave. were 20th centuryites."[3]

Despite *Variety's* suggestion that this plot had lost its kick during the Gold Rush, it remained an absolute staple of early film imagery. For example, in "The Threshing Scene," filmed in 1905,[4] a henpecked husband tries, with limited success, to kill himself. His wife (played by a man), a large woman with a dark hair bun and ringlet curls hanging down the side of her face, easily brings to mind the notoriously asexual old maid. As the film opens, the husband is sitting peacefully in his chair smoking a pipe. His shrewish wife repeatedly disturbs him with demands that he perform various household chores. In despair, he tries to end his life, first by breathing gas from the lamp, then by drinking poison, finally by hanging himself. Each attempt is thwarted by the intervening wife, who finally causes his death when she scolds him angrily over his suicide attempts. The fact that it is the wife's harassment that kills him indicates that marriage truly strips men of power—even the power to do away with themselves.

This theme is repeated and amplified in G. W. Bitzer's compli-cated "Trial Marriages," released in 1907.[5] Satirizing both "free love"—the craze that advocated sexual partnership without marriage (hence "Trial Marriage")—and the marriage "problem" so debated in the press, this clever film offered the expected conclusions. In the opening scene, a well-heeled gentleman laughs at a news article ad-vocating trial marriages. The scoffing comes back to haunt him in the various scenes that follow. In "His First Trial—The Crying Girl," a young woman cries all the time. Her father wants to know why she cries and, assuming that her husband is the reason, beats him up. In "He Meets A Peach—The Jealous Girl," the young lovers are sweet and cooing until marriage. Then the new bride growls and attacks her husband when he pays too much attention to the servant girl. "While There's Life There's Hope—The Tired Girl," the third section, plays upon the henpecked-husband theme. The wife, too tired to do any-thing, sleeps while her husband cleans, prepares meals, and serves her. Finally, while doing the dishes, he breaks some in order to awaken her, then forces an apron on her. In retaliation she orders him to do "man's work" and carry a heavy bucket of dirt from the basement. When it falls on him, she laughs. The husband is damned again in "In Union There Is Strength." In this scene, he marries a woman with five little hellions. When he attempts to discipline them, his bride attacks him. "Trial Marriages" closes with "Never Again," the vow the man makes as he lies in the hospital, bruised and beaten.

This ten-minute film, quite lengthy for 1907, deploys all the usual images of marital unhappiness while making a pun on the notion of trial marriages—a fairly radical concept. These marriages are indeed trials to the men involved. Romantic love appears only in "The Jealous Girl," and disappears immediately upon marriage, at which point the husband's attention wanders to the servant girl. Once again, marriage removes desire and inevitably displaces it onto another single woman.

Films about husbands who found their sexual pleasure in the household maid constituted their own genre, including "The Wrath of a Jealous Wife"[6] (1903) and "A Gay Old Boy" (produced originally in 1899 but not released until 1903).[7] "The Wrath of a Jealous Wife" has a self-explanatory plot. A middle-class couple eats dinner, and the wife leaves for a moment; when the maid comes in to clear the table, the husband pulls her onto his lap, and they kiss and fondle each other. The wife returns, grabs the maid by the ear, and hauls her off the husband's lap. Then she chases him around the table, throwing plates and food at him. Eventually, the wife gets her husband down, sits on him, and pounds his head on the floor. In a similar scene from "A Gay Old Boy," the maid is reluctant when the husband grabs her and fights him off. Philosophical about the rejection, he sits down to read, but when his wife enters the room she somehow surmises what has happened, takes her husband by the lapels, and begins throwing him around the room.

The twin themes of the husband's chasing the maid and his violent punishment at the hands of a browbeating wife provided early film audiences a comfortable familiarity. The viewer was supposed to sympathize with the unsuccessfully errant husband, whose "innocent" flirtations merely represent feeble attempts to regain his manhood. The manner of his asexual wife's retribution, a very physical beating, reminded everyone what was lacking in this marriage and what had been lost in the process.

The office, an emerging site of gender integration in this period, became a new setting for scenes of adultery. Instead of the upstairs maid, the unfulfilled male's eye turned to the new female secretary or stenographer. The identical themes appeared, demonstrating this particular marital vision's flexibility and staying power. "Mr. Gay and Mrs.," released in 1907, caught the transition from home to office rather well.[8] Initially, the errant husband is seen flirting with and kissing the maid, until Mrs. Gay catches them together. The next scene finds him at the office, engaging in similar shenanigans with his secretary, when his wife walks in, cuffs his ear, and yells at him. She next catches him hiding under a table at a restaurant, where he had been dining with the secretary. The wife responds by bringing him a new, "ugly" secretary (a man dressed as a woman) the next day. The husband fires the new secretary, brings back the old one, and provides her with makeup so that she can look ugly if his wife comes. The final fight, at home, features more yelling and chasing, and the husband ends up locked into the Murphy bed.

In "The Masher," from 1910,[9] a woman berates her rather sour-looking husband after he makes eyes at a young woman strolling by.

Stalking off to sulk, he spies a woman dressed like his wife and throws himself on her to beg forgiveness. Horrified, the woman alerts passersby, who chase the derelict husband. In the meantime the wife is accosted by a masher. She contacts the police, who offer her a description of a man (her husband) they have just caught for a similar crime. She goes to the police station to make an identification. There, she meets the woman her husband accosted, and they bond. When the husband is brought out, she demands that the police lock him up and throw away the key. The two women then shake hands triumphantly, cementing their connection. If the plot tied them together through shared victimization and triumph, the film did so in a more interesting symbolic fashion. The woman dressed identically to the wife is unmistakably marked as the "old maid," both in physical presentation and in her resistance to sexual approach. That she is dressed in precisely the same outfit as the wife—that she is "mistaken" for the wife and then bonds with her—hardly seems coincidental. Old maids and wives thus share a common denominator: both are desexualized figures mocked for their absence from the world of desire. Precisely "twinned" in "The Masher," the equation of the old maid to the wife could not be made more directly—or missed by any audience.

In early films, married women almost never find sexual satisfaction—even when they seek it. Consider, for example, the imagery for female adultery. Male adultery played as comic relief in these films, but when women strayed, the text became more melodramatic, the context tragic. Wives found themselves caught in a double-bind in these films. "Proper" wives had no sexuality, and their husbands always looked elsewhere. "Improper" wives, characterized as women who demonstrated sexual desire, could only express that desire through adultery, ensuring their disgrace.

Numerous films portrayed the adulterous woman whose actions destroy her life. "The Unfaithful Wife,"[10] a relatively long 1903 film with several "chapters," offered the full tragic tableau. In the chapter entitled "The Lover," a very proper-looking woman (in a clearly middle-class setting, with the prerequisite piano and parlor) entertains a male visitor who holds her hand and strokes her fingers as they engage in intimate conversation. Another man, clearly the husband, enters and begins to quarrel with the lover. The wife stops the fray and, after the lover leaves, turns her back on her husband, nonchalantly picking up a magazine. In part two, "The Fight,"[11] the woman has run off and become a dance-hall girl. She is sitting with her well-dressed lover in a bar when the husband arrives. The two men fight, and the husband gets the worst of it while his wife looks on with complete disinterest. She pays for her lack of remorse or concern in the final episode, "Murder and Suicide."[12] She and her husband enter the parlor of their home together. Her clothing is torn and off her shoulder—an implication of sexual activity. He flies into a rage and, in a remarkably graphic and violent scene for the period, attempts to strangle her as they struggle over a gun. He throws her to the floor; as she falls, he shoots her three times.

"The Unfaithful Wife" was an early and somewhat anomalous portrayal of female infidelity. The violence is particularly intense and perhaps too realistic. Later films offered hope of redemption and painted their wayward females as troubled but salvageable rather than as wanton women devoid of conscience. D. W. Griffith had a great hand in developing these films. In "The Message" and "The Better Way,"[13] both from 1909, Griffith presented themes of adultery, separation, and reconciliation. "The Message" depicts a woman who has married into the hard-working life of the farm. Bored, she runs off with a dandy who used to woo her. As she happily packs, she sees her little child and cries out, "How could I leave you?" She does leave, but the child follows. The woman, clearly distraught over her decision, joins her beau, but as he fetches a taxi to take them away, the child arrives, and the mother returns home. She tells her noble husband all and begs forgiveness. "The Better Way" offers a similar story but is set as a period piece, with Pilgrims as the main characters. In this film, a woman is loved by two men. She chooses and marries one but is still in love with the other. The other suitor continues his advances and finally persuades the woman to run away with him. But her conscience betrays her, and she returns to her parents' home. They bring her to her husband, who, naturally, forgives her.

In these sentimentalized portraits, female temptation was neither funny nor "natural." The wife's return, particularly to motherhood, stabilized the paternal authority of the family, so the husband could afford to be generous and forgiving. Real-life dramas, however, did not always work out so tidily. Large numbers of women left marriages for various purposes, but particularly in pursuit of sexual pleasure. The inevitable on-screen depiction of their return—the flip side of the comedic dynamic that located departure and sexuality as male prerogatives—expressed both male desire and male anxiety over a perceived loss of power.

Although these films portrayed with great gusto marriages in disarray, they dealt gingerly with actual divorce. Given the growing number of divorces and the concurrent public outcry, the subject could not be completely avoided, but the controversy surrounding it restrained popular treatment to a certain degree. Marriage was a longstanding target of popular humor, but widespread divorce had arrived too recently and represented too disturbing an alteration in the social fabric to withstand serious satirical attacks. How the humor could be best offered remained a subject under negotiation, as did a common sensibility about the positive and negative effects of divorce. Though jokes were made, caution clearly prevailed, particularly in early film.

Vaudeville proved less circumspect. Such titles as "Wanted, A Divorce" (a satire on the earlier, much-performed "Wanted, A Husband"), "A Matrimonial Mix-Up" (which played in San Jose, California, in 1906), and "A Matrimonial Blizzard" ("based upon a married couple applying to the same attorney for a divorce over fancied grievances"), were all standard fare for vaudeville patrons in the early years of the century.[14] By 1912 the *Boston Herald* could review May Tully's sketch "The Battle Cry of Freedom" with the simple comment: "a one act comedy that deals with Reno, Nevada or what amounts to the same thing—divorce."[15]

The raucous and vicious tone in vaudeville attests to the intensity created by this turn-of-the-century emotional tussle. One popular song from 1906, ad-libbed each night by the famous vaudevillian Harry Bulgur and recorded by an unknown reporter, had audiences in stitches:

A friend of mine he took a wife, she scolded from the start
But there isn't anything that can't be cured
He didn't want to take her life, he had a tender heart
And besides he knew that she was not insured.

While passing by a drugstore an electric belt he saw
He took it home and with it belted wifey in the jaw:
She never scolded him again but went home to her Ma
There isn't anything that can't be cured.

CHORUS: Oh joy, no lectures to annoy
He's all alone, but that can be endured
His wife's gone home to Mother
And he's looking for another
But there isn't anything that can't be cured.[16]

Harry Bulgur might sing of hitting wifey in the jaw to force her
out, but D. W. Griffith would never depict such a scene on film.
Although the miserable men in films about marriage usually stayed
that way, their strongest desires thwarted by female power, depictions of divorce did finally emerge. The cinematic sources on divorce
in this period are tainted by reform ideology, because Griffith, the
most important filmmaker after 1908, flooded the screen with "acceptable" narratives. Few films dealt with divorce directly, and when
Griffith produced movies on this theme, he gave them the same sentimental tint that colored so many of his epics.

Two examples of Griffith's handiwork exemplify his sentimentalized response to divorce. "And A Little Child Shall Lead Them"
(1909) and "A Child's Stratagem" (1910) both address divorce from
the child's point of view.[17] The first film takes place after one child in
the family has died and the two parents, in the process of splitting
apart, ignore the remaining child. In one scene, the two squabble
while the little girl, toy in hand, tries to interest one of them in playing with her. Finally, the parents notice the tortured youngster, realize the error of their ways, and reconcile. In "A Child's Stratagem,"
the devastated child is more aggressive about preventing her parents'
upcoming divorce. She fakes a kidnapping, leaving a ransom note,
and then heads to a relative's to wait. En route she becomes lost, and
a genuine crisis ensues. She is finally returned by kind strangers, and
her parents reconcile in gratitude.

Earlier films were less sentimental. "The Divorce," a surprisingly
detailed 1903 effort by G. W. Bitzer (better known for his light comedies) offered a starkly realistic portrait in three chapters.[18] In the first
part, "Detected," an envelope falls from the husband's pocket when

he changes coats. His wife reads the letter after he's gone. Shocked, she falls into a chair, cradling her head, then leaves the room. The next scene, "On the Trail," shows the wife visiting a detective agency and hiring an operative to get the goods on her (apparently) philandering husband. In the final part, "Evidence Secured," a sordid scene of illicit relations is depicted. A waiter delivers liquor to a hotel room occupied by the husband and a woman in a dressing gown. The wife and detective wander through the hotel peering in keyholes until the detective finds the right room. He has the wife look, and she faints in horror. After she comes to, they force the door open to confront the pair.

Uncharacteristically, the film took the female character's point of view. Though it replicated the middle-class propaganda of male lust and female asexuality, "The Divorce" found fault with the philandering husband. Even films about women generally stood apart from them, as if in observation. Yet in "The Divorce," with the exception of the short expository portion in the third act, the audience sees only what the woman sees (an effect that is particularly pronounced in the keyhole scene). It is clear that the divorce will be initiated by the lead character on the basis of the discovered adultery, reflecting at least one major ground for which women actually filed for divorce. Although the film reinforced stereotypes of female asexuality and passivity in the marital equation, it provided a more complicated representation of divorce and one that held within it more components of the contemporary controversy than did the later Griffith epics.

However, "The Divorce" could hardly be called representative of how early film depicted the issue. Much more common were witty knockoffs such as "Why Mr. Nation Wants A Divorce,"[19] whose themes bore little relation to actual divorce issues raised in the courts. (For example, in real male-initiated divorces, alcohol addiction was a common accusation hurled at the defendant wife.) Though the film's comedic tone stood in direct contrast to the reality of divorce in 1901 America, its vision of a family broken up by female aggressiveness was not inappropriate, given the fact that women requested most divorces. Such films probably provide a relatively accurate barometer of popular male sentiment about divorce at the turn of the century.[20]

Early films dealing with marriage reoriented the arguments so as to blunt the assault upon male prerogative. In the comedies, humorously tortured men desperately sought escape from lifeless marriages. They created humor by inverting notions of the way men "ought" to be at a time when many had no idea how to define such things anymore. Challenges to gender and sexuality permeated the culture, and an exploding divorce rate driven primarily by women elevated those challenges into an attack on the seat of patriarchal authority—the family. The sexual problems in marriage had to be represented as products of female asexuality in order to thwart the actual challenge to male power posed by changing marital codes.

III

This struggle to understand what was happening to marital relations existed in an even more contentious fashion in courts and communities across the country. In the "real" world, which could not be neatly ordered by the all-powerful filmmaker, women filed for more than two-thirds of all divorces, and they spoke their rage with unmuted voices. Attempts to make sense of this incomprehensible phenomenon took place in newspapers, community forums, and political platforms. Opponents of divorce called for restrictive action and even federal laws to restrain it; social scientists and public philosophers countered that divorce was a positive change that freed individuals to pursue happiness.[21]

The first objective evidence of rising divorce rates appeared in the Department of Labor's 1889 statistical survey on the subject. Covering the years 1867 to 1886, the report indicated a strong increase in the frequency of divorces. Although the absolute number of divorces—25,535 in 1886—was relatively small, it represented a 150 percent increase over the 1867 figure. Adjusting for population growth did not significantly diminish the dramatic increase.[22]

As disturbing as this trend was to many, it was nothing compared to what followed in the next twenty years. Though divorce was also on the rise throughout western Europe, the United States easily outdistanced the competition. In 1910, Switzerland had the highest divorce rate in Europe, with 0.4 divorces per thousand population; the

U.S. rate was the highest in the world, 0.9 per thousand at the beginning of World War I. Rate per thousand population is a somewhat misleading statistic, as it lumps married with nonmarried individuals. An even more revealing statistic is the divorce rate per thousand marriages. In 1910, that rate stood at 4.5 per thousand in the United States. Social observers could still point to the raw figures—83,045 total divorces in 1910—to demonstrate that the problem was not dangerously widespread. Certainly the numbers seem small compared to today's totals. However, divorce opponents saw the writing on the wall in these ever-increasing numbers and anticipated the future with extraordinary accuracy.[23]

Felix Adler, noted reformer and founder of the ethical culture movement, decried marriage's decline. He bemoaned as early as 1905 "the modern view . . . as preached in Ibsen's *Nora,*" viewing it to be "anarchical and mad" because it permitted a "man and a woman to go to the marriage altar oblivious of the very object for which marriage is instituted, assuming that it is a delightful contrivance for making their hearts warm." Adler blamed the "evil of divorce" on the fact that such individuals had forgotten that "they are servants, that there are great social ends to which they must bow."[24] Railing against the winds of change, Adler put his finger on the problem of the new marriage. He saw "comradeship" between the sexes as "pernicious" and "obnoxious and antagonistic to the idea of marriage," stating: "Such a thing as a permanent comradeship cannot be imposed. In the very nature of comradeship is implied the possibility of separation . . . *Comradeship depends on free choice and free choice can be annulled* [emphasis added]. There is nothing permanent in the idea of comradeship."[25] This well-publicized 1905 attack revealed just how radical emerging marriage ideals seemed to be and how great a threat they posed to the traditional view of marriage. Adler was correct; marriage did cease to become a permanent bond, and on precisely the grounds he feared. As men and women looked to each other for friendship in marriage, they created the possibility of finding those connections elsewhere.

By the 1920s, the so-called "companionate marriage," documented by numerous historians, had taken its place as an icon of American social stability.[26] The concept of friendship in marriage and the phrase "companionate marriage" danced around the actual topic of this discourse. The clear subtext—and sometimes the actual text—of this controversial conversation on comradeship between the genders was the sexual practice engaged in by husband and wife. Though much marriage literature in the 1920s emphasized being "pals," the real friendship was to occur in the bedroom. The focus on nonreproductive sexuality and friendship between husbands and wives restructured the public imperative for marriage. Personal satisfaction came to be perceived as a positive competitive value to social order. The concept of personal satisfaction, even "happiness," was far more subjective than earlier definitions of marriage; unmoored from these traditional foundations by the early twentieth century, ideas about marriage have drifted quite dramatically ever since.

The companionate marriage was but one component of the turn-of-the-century transformation that eventually encoded sexual desire into the public representation of the self. Marriage became a particularly significant location for attention because it occupied the central position in the discourse that attempted to contain sexuality. Though it was far from the only locus, as the dominant structure for social control of sexual practice it was a pivotal one. Yet the marriage system that accentuated the sexual relationship between the two parties did not achieve primacy in a simple fashion.

The tales told in the personal disasters outlined in divorce depositions revealed the centrality of nonreproductive sex to the turn-of-the-century marriage. The willingness to dissolve a union over this issue demonstrated the newly privileged, publicly acknowledged status for sexuality in marriage. Although this centrality existed to some degree among white middle-class couples in the late nineteenth century,[27] divorce records in Sacramento make clear that by the dawn of the twentieth century individuals throughout the community looked to marital sex for personal gratification. This understanding formed the basis for common standards of sexual expectation that transcended class. The discourse about sexuality took on a highly public character, as once-private negotiations over desire formed the core of a newly defined social goal for marriage.

While the Felix Adlers expounded and the filmmakers exploited, most of this redefinition worked itself out in hundreds of thousands of divorce cases. These open, ferocious arguments shattered the stylized rhetoric on the "true" nature of marriage. The personal negotiations in which marital partners engaged inevitably became community contests, if not in detail then at least in gross form. The disputes and, to some degree, the resolutions involved in these cases became the basis for an emerging public dialogue on the nature not only of marriage but of overall relations between the genders.

Those filing for divorce in Sacramento at the turn of the century did so with the sure knowledge that their marriage would end. Although contemporary commentators, appalled by rising divorce rates, urged jurisdictions to clamp down and deny the petitions, Sacramento residents faced no such obstacles. In this, they stood with many throughout the country. Though some states sought to tighten grounds for divorce and stem the tide, their efforts had no significant impact on divorce rates nationwide.[28] Western states are often presumed to have been "divorce mills," largely because Nevada created laws designed to attract the divorce trade as early as 1900. However, western states' divorce rates only marginally exceeded those in the rest of the country. If western states often granted divorces to individuals who had been married elsewhere, one need only look at the overall breakdown of population for an explanation. The 1900 census demonstrates that large majorities of the population in the frontier states had migrated from other areas. Naturally, divorce rates reflected that reality. Disapproving easterners attempted to claim that eased residency requirements made western states divorce havens. However, with the exception of Nevada, western states had lax residency requirements to facilitate settlement and civic growth, not to encourage divorce. When some states, under pressure from reformers, altered their residency requirements after 1900, divorce rates remained unaffected.[29]

Although the demographic data show that western divorces seemed to involve migratory couples, Sacramento divorce records actually reflect a more stable population. The vast majority of those divorced in Sacramento had been married there or in a neighboring California community.[30] Overwhelmingly, those who sought divorce in Sacramento had lived there for many years, married there, worked there, and saw in their town a stable community that would support them in their desire to escape from an unacceptable domestic situation. Their assumptions proved correct. Divorce applicants generally received sympathetic hearings and, with extremely rare exception, speedy separations from their spouses.

In Sacramento, as in the rest of the country, women usually initiated the marital break. In 1895 women filed 89 percent of the divorce requests. By 1905 more men had joined the parade, but still more than 72 percent of Sacramento divorces were filed by women.[31] In this respect the town exceeded the national trend, which showed that two-thirds of all divorces filed were brought by women at the turn of the century.[32] Marriage seemed no more or less stable in Sacramento than anywhere else. Separations occurred after as little as four months and as long as thirty years.[33] Little difference is evident between the stories told in 1895 and those revealed ten years later; rather, it is their similarities that strike the reader immediately. Depositions from divorce proceedings show that views of marriage that had emerged by the late nineteenth century only deepened their hold on the American social imagination as time passed. The testimony illustrates not only the sadness of those seeking marital dissolution but also the traumas faced by any two people attempting to make common union in the new climate of personal relations.

One particularly evocative case offers not only a capsule picture of sexual standards in marriage but also the degree to which new ways of understanding marital problems emerged under court pressure. Although somewhat unusual because no divorce was granted, the case is enlightening nonetheless. *Riley v. Riley* dragged on for eleven years as the pair repeatedly tried to escape each other.[34] They began their attempt to separate in 1895 and left an extraordinary record of their relationship. Ultimately the judge forced these two miserable individuals to remain together, but their legal trail reveals key information about the sexual expectations, responsibilities, and negotiations that had begun to mark late-nineteenth-century relationships.

Ella and James Riley married in 1884 and despite religious differences seemed to have a successful marriage. Ella, a Protestant, promised to convert to James's Catholicism and to raise any children as good Catholics. The couple had no children, however, and Ella Riley, after attending church for several years, discontinued worship in 1891. At that time, the situation between the two began rapidly to deteriorate.

The Rileys' specific legal maneuverings signal the intensity of their difficulties. Ella Riley filed the initial complaint and charged her husband with cruelty, a standard ground for divorce. James, she claimed, was cold and verbally abusive. James Riley filed a cross-complaint charging Ella with cruelty and requesting a divorce. This counter-charge alone marked the case as atypical; defendants in divorce suits, usually men, tended to default. By refusing to answer, the husband generally guaranteed that the divorce went through with little difficulty, suggesting some level of collusion, spoken or unspoken, between the parties. When the defendant did respond to the suit, it was usually to request that the plaintiff's divorce request be denied. These responses generally claimed innocence of all accusations and urged that the marriage be maintained. However, such requests were routinely ignored and rarely dissuaded judges from granting dissolution. James, however, wanted out of this marriage as much as Ella did, and his countersuit indicates the presence of particularly hard feelings. He not only demanded a divorce but insisted that it be granted with his version of the story supported by the court, his private agony and his wife's humiliation exposed to public view.

If James Riley was "disagreeable . . . to an extent that was almost unbearable to a woman of any affection or sensitive feelings,"[35] Ella Riley had "never, at any time, . . . allowed [James] to have full and complete sexual intercourse with her."[36] These two charges served as the basis for the complaint and cross-complaint. James Riley made no attempt to deflect the claim made against him by pointing to his own charge; no cause and effect were discussed or presumed. Rather, the pair acted as if (and the court seemed to agree) two separate problems afflicted this marriage, each carrying its own significant weight.

The judge found each charge supported by evidence and sufficient to grant a divorce. With respect to Ella Riley's claim, it was enough that James Riley "seldom, if ever, spoke a kind or pleasant word to her, though he was pleasant and courteous to most of the people who visited his house." The fact that "when she would ask him a respectful question, he would, in a harsh, rude and cruel manner tell her that if she wished to know to go and find out, that he was not her news-carrier" constituted sufficient assault on a middle-class woman's tender sensibilities to warrant marital dissolution. James insulted his wife's friends by arguing over religion and let her know that he would not let her into his room even if he were dying. After refusing "for a number of years . . . without any just cause, . . . to accompany the plaintiff to any place of amusement," James Riley began to disappear for extended periods until finally, in April 1895, he moved out for good.[37] The judge commented in his lengthy ruling

[t]hat the plaintiff is a woman of a good deal of affection, refinement and sensitiveness, which fact was also well known to the defendant, and such treatment by the defendant of her, did cause the plaintiff great mental suffering, anguish and sorrow, and did impair and injure her physical health, and often caused her to weep to the extent that she was not in proper condition to receive her friends when they called upon her, and for about two years, in consequence of such treatment by the defendant, her sleep was disturbed and she did not enjoy a good night's rest.[38]

The judge, having heard the testimony, concluded that it was "clearly sufficient to support a judgment of divorce based upon the ground of cruel treatment."[39]

And yet the court could not grant the plaintiff's request. Citing California case law that "it is eminently fit that he who seeks a divorce should himself be guiltless of conduct which would entitle the other party to similar relief,"[40] the judge began an extended exploration of Ella Riley's behavior in the marriage. Utilizing the defendant's cross-complaint as a basis, the court, relying upon "a great deal of testimony, . . . much of which is conflicting and irreconcilable, and much of it also of a very offensive nature,"[41] detailed what it perceived to be Ella Riley's sexual dysfunction.

Mrs. Riley was, according to the court, apparently a healthy woman; she did suffer from some minor back problems, but none severe enough to "prevent her from copulating with the defendant."[42] Despite this, she "refused . . . to permit defendant to have full intercourse with her; but would pull away from him and . . . thus destroy all pleasure or effect of cohabitation."[43] The court cited testimony that "frequently when the defendant was trying to have sexual intercourse with her, she would become hysterical and go into spasms."[44] The court was satisfied that medical advice had been properly sought. The family doctor testified that she was "afected [*sic*] with a spasmodic affliction"[45] but that Mrs. Riley "could be safely and successfully treated."[46] The physician warned, however, "that she never could enjoy sexual intercourse unless she was so treated and that the manner which she had sexual intercourse with the defendant was injurious to the health of both of them."[47]

Ella Riley refused to accept treatment for her sexual "disability," thereby providing James Riley with the means for a successful counterclaim. Citing "Brown on Divorce 186," the judge ruled that "[a] refusal to be cured, unless the case would involve an operation dangerous to the person's life or health, or which would be of doubtful efficacy, of an impediment to proper sexual intercourse, is a ground for divorce."[48]

With that finding, the divorce was doomed. Even though such an interpretation rarely appeared in 1895 Sacramento divorce courts, the judge ruled that "the evidence submitted by both parties is sufficient to support a decree of divorce, but as neither came into court with clean hands, and as both are at fault, each of their prayers for divorce must be denied."[49] The Rileys remained trapped together in mutual anguish.

The Rileys' unclean hands were muddied in ways that apparently could not be addressed by the court directly. The judge, for example, did not rule upon the merit of James Riley's complaint that his wife did not wish to have children and that this decision prompted her refusal to permit complete intercourse. The court stood unmoved by Ella Riley's concerns about pregnancy. Her claim to her husband that if she got "in a family way she would have a criminal operation committed upon herself to get rid of it"[50] seemed to have been viewed as an incomprehensible aberration. Noted the puzzled judge, "The only reason that she assigned why she refused the defendant to have proper sexual intercourse with her, and why she refused to be treated, was that she feared that if she did, she would become pregnant and would bear children, which might cause her death; but there was no good reason why she should have feared any danger."[51] Mrs. Riley's attempts to control her reproductive functions were perceived as a symptom of sexual pathology.

The description of Ella Riley's "dysfunction" offered to the court consisted largely of her demanding her husband's withdrawal—the single most common form of birth control in the late nineteenth century. It is somewhat surprising that this was not discussed more directly. It should be noted that the "fear of death" argument offered by Ella Riley might well have been disingenuous. Anyone willing to risk an illegal abortion, truly a dangerous procedure in 1895 Sacramento, had more complicated motives than a simple fear of dying in childbirth. Her husband implied that she had political goals as well and that she was working with a group known as the "APAs."[52] It is possible that she wanted to avoid revealing her sympathies and potential involvement in illegal activities, such as the promotion of birth control, lest these bring about an unfavorable court ruling on her divorce request. Such speculation does not make her stated rationale any less powerful; like many women of her generation, she probably factored a variety of issues and concerns into her thoughts on having children.

Ella Riley's spasmodic condition also merits closer evaluation. James Riley complained that his wife had two sexual problems, which he viewed as related. His wife did not permit him "to have full connection with her when cohabiting," and she tended to "go into spasms" when he attempted intercourse at other times. He found "her actions on such occasions . . . unpleasant, disagreeable, and disgusting." It "caused him to lose all pleasure," and eventually he felt compelled to sleep elsewhere because he could not stand the sight of her.[53] It was this "spasmodic affliction" for which he sought a physician's counsel. Riley's complaint, upheld by the court, alleged that the doctor told her "that she needed treatment therefore and that if she was not treated from said affliction, it would be impossible to enjoy said sexual intercourse with her."[54] In other words, unless she was "cured," James Riley would be unable to achieve sexual pleasure.

The specifics of Ella Riley's spasmodic affliction are, not surprisingly, shrouded in a certain level of vagueness. Although the condition is referred to repeatedly in the defendant's cross-complaint and

definitely constitutes a separate issue from her refusal to permit him
to "complete" intercourse, it is unclear whether Mrs. Riley's spasms
began as James Riley attempted intercourse or in the midst of climax.
This is not an irrelevant interpretative point but indeed goes to the
heart of sexual expectations and assumptions about the nature of sexual desire and response in men and women in turn-of-the-century
society.

If Ella Riley's spasms occurred as intercourse began, then she apparently placed some form of conscious or unconscious restrictions
on sexual activity. If, however, her spasms were a form of sexual response, then both James Riley and the physician remained conflicted
as to the nature of appropriate female sexual behavior—a subject of
not-inconsiderable debate during the period. A third possibility exists
as well. Some professionals believed that spasms during intercourse
interfered with conception. According to one standard text published
in 1891, "voluptuous spasms" caused a weakness and repose that actually served to produce infertility.[55] If Ella Riley was politically active in the birth control movement, as her husband suspected, she
would have been aware of this theory, and her spasms might represent another attempt at contraception.

Ella Riley's specific problem will remain a mystery, but the questions raised by the testimony in the Riley divorce are less obtuse.
Many couples faced precisely the same set of problems as they negotiated terms of sexuality and reproduction, methods of birth control,
and definitions of sexual satisfaction. This was clearly a long-standing
issue between the Rileys and one that had forced them into repeated
confrontation over an eleven-year period. The acknowledgment of
their disagreement and inability to reconcile the two positions had
sent them into the medical community for assistance.

When the physician found a pathology in Ella Riley's control over
sexual behavior, he simultaneously forged links with both the past
and the future. Ella Riley's refusal to engage in intercourse as defined
by her husband's enjoyment could be pathologized in a nineteenth-
century vision that saw female sexuality as an aspect of reproduction
and male sexuality as a component of pleasure. Conversely, the med-
icalizing of Mrs. Riley's sexual behavior, and the introduction of a
physician's diagnosis into court in order to justify legal decisions,

demonstrates a more modern sensibility. The twentieth century saw the newly professionalized worlds of law and medicine become integrated and applied to sexuality.

The Riley divorce well demonstrates the degree to which marital sexuality had begun to occupy a variety of new and important discursive spaces at the turn of the century. Medical science provided an extensive and profound new set of definitions by which individuals could recast their understandings of marriage and sex. Legal analysis in divorce proceedings reshaped these questions again. Equally important was the willingness of the two parties to a divorce to engage in an extremely public discussion, one involving both friends and acquaintances, with a permanent written record. Divorce court opened sexual choices in marriage to public scrutiny and social evaluation.

Paradoxical results emerged from that kind of scrutiny. On one hand, the increased role of the courts propelled a dramatic growth in legal and medical authority over sexual definition; on the other hand, rising divorce rates reinforced an ever more eccentric personalized sexuality. The more divorce cases illuminated a variety of sexual choices and disagreements, the more people began to understand sexuality as an individualized phenomenon. Cases such as the Rileys' provided individuals with a window through which to witness differing sexual practice, inevitably forcing a reevaluation of their own.

The Rileys' divorce illustrates the kind of internal conversations that had begun to dominate late-nineteenth-century marriages. The nature and quality of sexual practice, as well as its relationship to reproduction, were topics that had to be dealt with directly. Such discussions may well have contrasted with contemporary public imagery and, indeed, probably helped change it. Though many couples successfully worked out a variety of contraceptive solutions, including coitus interruptus, the Rileys were not able to do so, and their public dispute on the topic leaves solid evidence as to the terms of the debate.

Such cases made marriage an open terrain for both scrutiny and an imposition of interpretation. The medical and legal communities saw Ella Riley's behavior within the context of female asexuality, a not unnatural assumption for 1895. Yet they were deeply troubled by the complications in this case. Though asexuality in a middle-class woman could not be considered pathological, her refusal to be "cured" and perform marital duties seemed incomprehensible. Ella Riley's highly political understanding of sexual activity and her attack on the patriarchal family structure could not be more clear, yet it left the court completely befuddled. Like the filmmakers whose products emerged soon after, doctors and lawyers as early as 1895 were attempting to contain and contextualize the emerging female attitude toward marriage within the boundaries of known sensibilities. These newly professionalized voices of male authority searched for a way to reconstitute local patriarchal control as women asserted increasing independence within marital confines.

"Cruelty" was the accusation often hurled at such women, and the introduction of this language helped reshape marital values. Many who supported divorce cast it as an element of a kinder, gentler world. Marriages could be harsh, and cruelty should be abhorred in a civilized society. Though the most complicated and ambiguous ground for divorce, the charge of cruelty offered the best possibility of success for each party. Over time it grew in definition to encompass an extraordinarily rich diversity of meanings. Simultaneously, that expansion cemented the idea that cruelty might exist inherently within the fundamental construction of marriage.[56]

The continuous stream of examples included repeated testimony alleging sexual abuse, both verbal and physical. The public airing of sexual dirty laundry in divorce depositions was dramatic enough, but the collapsing of sexual behavior with charges of cruelty reshaped the way in which sexuality in marriage would be defined and socially received. Those producing community standards identified cruelty with violent rape and seduction, the emerging Progressive bugaboo.[57] With divorce testimony however, ongoing practices in sanctioned sexual relationships began to be seen as cruel. "Cruelty" thus left the world of deviancy and criminality and entered the language of normative heterosexual desire.

Men who initiated divorce suits postulated definitions of cruelty that applied to daily sexual life. The sexual injuries they claimed included both the humiliation they felt when their wives rejected them as well as actual adultery these women committed. John Stoll complained that his wife, Ursula, "declined to eat at the same table, . . . refused to associate with him, neglected him constantly, has held herself aloof from him for days and weeks at a time, and . . . has refused him the attentions of a wife."[58] Mild-mannered Mr. Morten was only married for four months before he filed for divorce, despairing that the "defendant found fault with the plaintiff's mother and made derogatory remarks of the influence plaintiff's mother had with him." Believing himself to be of a "mild contented and affectionate disposition," Morten was taken aback by the speed with which his marriage disintegrated. "Ever since the marriage . . . the defendant has constantly impressed upon plaintiff her disregard for him and her discontent of her married life with plaintiff."[59] Apparently the judge agreed, and their short marriage, which began on the first day of 1905, was dissolved by mid-May. Sylvia Landes's "extreme cruelty" to her husband, Charles, involved visiting the carnival when it came to town and being seen publicly with "a total stranger called 'the Turk'" who had "care of certain camels." Mrs. Landes "publicly hung around and flirted with said stranger, visited soda water stands with him and was treated to soda water by him and sat beside him in the swing . . ."[60] Charles Landes's "great humiliation" over this and similar accusations drove him to end his eighteen-month marriage.

The relationship between sexuality and cruelty rested on a deeply gender-based set of assumptions. A close reading of divorce documents yields clues as to the presumptions held by members of each sex. Both men and women ultimately furthered the idea that cruelty was a potential aspect of everyday marital relations. Moreover, when partners began to define certain behaviors as excessively cruel—sufficient to dissolve the relationship—inevitably a definition of "acceptable" cruelty followed. Withdrawal was a common theme for men, even beyond the particulars of the Riley case. Almost all men who initiated divorces accused their wives of engaging in both physical and sexual distancing. John Stoll's complaint about his wife's refusing to eat with him could be topped by W. N. Morris, whose wife would eat with him but refused to pass the salt.[61] Joseph Riley claimed that Ella Riley referred to him as a "thing" and spoke about him to others in his presence.[62] It seems unlikely that every couple who had little social interaction divorced. This was, after all, still at the tail end of an era marked by fairly strict homosocial divisions. Yet men uniformly characterized their wives' personal disaffection in both home space and the community as sexual distance. In fact, the silence at the dinner table detailed in these depositions came to symbolize silence in the bedroom. In these depositions we can easily see the roots to this common twentieth-century metaphor.

The equation of personal public coldness with sexual distance and cruelty says something direct about male expectation and underlying shifting cultural sensibilities. In part this shift represents an abrogation of the nineteenth-century model of marital duty; the incorporation of public behavior provides clues to the emerging affective paradigm, which has been documented by other historians of late-Victorian marriage.[63] This collapsing of public and private behavior became a major component of the modern marriage.

An explicit rejection of female passionlessness pervades these men's complaints. It was not simply that their wives would not permit them sexual access but that they would not provide love and emotional comfort, a prime element of which was sexual engagement. These men expected their wives to participate with eagerness; when they did not, and when their withdrawal became general, their actions were deemed to constitute cruelty of a distinctly sexual nature. However, there is little evidence that these women withdrew from their husbands out of an overarching lack of sexual desire; their coldness seems to have been aimed with precision at their husbands. For example, the Turk may have been the alternate recipient of Sylvia Landes's attention. Numerous other depositions testified to the charge of female adultery, indicating that these women were not tossing aside sexuality per se—only sex with their husbands. Neither the facts of these marriages as presented in courts nor the assumptions that mark them as "dysfunctional" support any commonly held belief that women were asexual creatures.

When women claimed cruelty, they usually testified to extraordinary physical brutality, but many complained of sexual mistreatment as well. This behavior usually took the form of accusations and, in the language of the time, "vile approbation" rather than physical violence. It is not surprising that what today's observers identify as sexual assault—coercive sex—rarely appeared in the depositions. The concept of marital rape is highly controversial even today, and at the turn of the century no such legal construct even existed. Undoubtedly, many marriages did include forced sexual encounters, but few attorneys would bother to have a client mention such an assault in her testimony. The concept of having marital sex against one's will not only had little value in terms of supporting appropriate grounds for divorce, it was simply inconceivable to most people. Though some forced sexual encounters do appear, more often a presumption of a "forced life," in which sexual assault is but one component, lies at the heart of these complaints.

Verbal assaults with a sexual text occupy an inordinate amount of space in these women's depositions. Men accused their wives regularly of nonspecific adultery with the proverbial milkman; direct, provable claims of adultery with a particular party were more rare. (Interestingly, the converse was true when women made such assertions against their husbands; such allegations almost always contained names, dates, and locations.) These accusations fell under the heading of verbal abuse—a component of the wife's cruelty complaint. According to many women, their husbands called them whores or prostitutes on a regular basis, whereas men charged that their wives referred to them as "whoremasters."[64] Women sometimes claimed that their husbands encouraged them to become prostitutes.[65] This jabbering appears frequently in divorce records and rarely served as the actual basis for divorce, leading one to speculate with some sense of certainty as to its presence in successful marriages as well.

Numerous examples point to the strikingly vicious sexual context of day-to-day conversation. When Hattie Mohwinkel, seventeen years old and pregnant, pleaded with her husband, John, not to walk out on her, he responded that "in the condition you are in you will be sucking my ass to get me home."[66] Thomas Harrison engaged in endless speculation on his wife's faithlessness with unusual specificity, identifying six men by name. Though he and his wife, Mary, had been married thirteen years and had two children, Harrison called her a "damned cat" and a "whore," claiming that "she was acting like a harlot," "getting up at night . . . and having intercourse with other men" in their home. Thomas repeatedly told their eldest daughter, "[T]hat is your mother, but I do not know whether I am your father or not." Mary Harrison finally gave up and filed for divorce after a visit from a

1a. *Top*, Barbershop customers happily anticipate the stocking-clad visitor . . .
1b. *Bottom*, . . . until they realize who it is. From "The Barber's Dee-light." This twist on "What Demoralized the Barbershop" forced audiences to reassess gender assumptions.

Julian Eltinge as the Bride and Groom.

2. A classic publicity shot for the *Julian Eltinge Magazine*, ca. 1913. Reproduced with permission of the Billy Rose Theatre Collection, The New York Public Library for the Performing Arts; Astor, Lenox and Tilsen Foundation.

The JULIAN ELTINGE COLD CREAM makes me look like these.

JULIAN ELTINGE
IN
"THE FASCINATING WIDOW"

3. Eltinge demonstrating his masculine and feminine versatility—as well as his ability to sell cold cream. Reproduced with permission of the Billy Rose Theatre Collection, The New York Public Library for the Performing Arts; Astor, Lenox and Tilsen Foundation.

4. Julian Eltinge, on the receiving end of a left jab, demonstrates his boxing skills (1917). Reproduced with permission of the Billy Rose Theatre Collection, The New York Public Library for the Performing Arts; Astor, Lenox and Tilsen Foundation.

5. Bothwell Browne plays with a sword in the flop "Miss Jack." Reproduced with permission of the Billy Rose Theatre Collection, The New York Public Library for the Performing Arts; Astor, Lenox and Tilsen Foundation.

6. Browne as a sultry Cleopatra in the scandalous "Serpent of the Nile."
Reproduced with permission of the Billy Rose Theatre Collection, The New York
Public Library for the Performing Arts; Astor, Lenox and Tilsen Foundation.

7 and 8. Playbill covers encouraged audiences' sexual imaginations. Reproduced with permission of the Billy Rose Theatre Collection, The New York Public Library for the Performing Arts; Astor, Lenox and Tilsen Foundation.

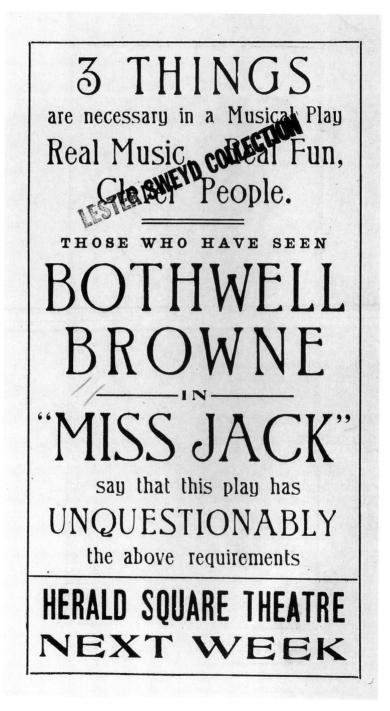

9. Advertising poster for Bothwell Browne's "Miss Jack." Reproduced with permission of the Billy Rose Theatre Collection, The New York Public Library for the Performing Arts; Astor, Lenox and Tilsen Foundation.

"reputable physician" led to accusations: "Immediately after the departure of the physician, the defendant, who had been present during all of the visit, accused . . . the physician of taking undue liberties." The imaginative defendant charged that "when the physician felt her pulse, . . . he squeezed her hand" and that "when he examined [her] condition . . . had passed his hand improperly over her body."[67]

The nastiness often got quite creative. William Harwood accused his wife, Ida, of having "gentlemen callers during his absence; that he could see their footprints in the yard, that he could see where they had climbed in the window, that he could see the prints of their boots on the bedstead." This imaginative miner also assumed his wife to be regularly pregnant, always by someone else, particularly her favorite cousin. He "did jeer . . . and say to her that the child would be freckled faced and red-headed just like her cousin Peck."[68] When Emma Malcolm asked her husband, Clarence, for money to buy clothing, he harangued, "[I]f you want any clothing, you will have to _____ for them (meaning for the plaintiff to know men carnally)." Clarence also told his wife frequently that he "would rather sleep with a China wench than with you."[69] According to Lucy Wing's 1905 divorce request, her husband, Frank, continuously accused her of adultery in front of their children, telling them that she was a "prostitute" and a "traitor," a "bad and lude [*sic*] woman." This behavior, coupled with Wing's solicitous inquiry into her health—"[H]ow is your heart, isn't it getting worse? You ought to be dead"—led Lucy Wing to get a divorce after twenty-six years.[70]

The definition of cruelty included a public aspect, as can be seen in Mary Elizabeth Grant's case. William Grant's sexual cruelty existed both in his adulterous actions and in the public retelling of his exploits. Grant not only contracted a venereal disease but also made a point of telling his wife's brother-in-law, Harry Snibly, that he was the father of a child in Reno by a Miss McDonald. Grant informed Snibly that he was "greatly enamored" of his mistress and chortled that "he had a 'bonanza' with her on the bench in the back yard of her residence and in secluded spots along the river." He admitted that he "had always been a 'chaser and always would be' or words to that effect." Snibly passed on the news to Mary Elizabeth, who firmly believed, according to her complaint, that her husband "well knew [this information] would be communicated . . . and was by him intended to inflict and did inflict . . . grievous mental suffering."[71]

Accusations of name-calling were as common in the female-initiated suits as charges of withdrawal were in the depositions filed by men. The comparison is appropriate. Both behaviors reflected the use of very specific sexual weapons; they were alternative, albeit gendered, facets of a similar phenomenon. Each party to the marriage identified a problem sexual area and used it to inflict injury. The "vile approbations" that men hurled at their wives focused the relationship on its sexual core. These assaults deployed sexually charged, socially unacceptable phrases to convey the anger in the marriage, reinforcing the idea that sexuality had become the central arena of contention in these marriages.

When a man called his wife a whore and a prostitute, he crossed numerous turn-of-the-century boundaries, at least insofar as Progressive rhetoric would have us understand family life. In that Progressive vision, men struggled in the savage marketplace outside the home while women maintained the moral order inside. Towns such as Sacramento might be seen as strongholds of such ideology. Certainly the courts, in granting divorces on the grounds of name-calling, attempted to maintain the social investment in that vision. Yet divorce testimony indicates that the ideology bore little resemblance to the truth of many people's lives; it underscores the degree to which the outside world had permeated the moral fabric of relations within the home. These "angels of the hearth" often found themselves accused of devilish transgressions. The whore/madonna dichotomy, supposedly so important to Victorian notions of womanhood, appeared in family conversations on a regular basis.

Sexual misbehavior and personal disagreement became conflated through such highly charged verbal contexts. It is not surprising that charges of prostitution and whoremastering appear so frequently. Prostitution occupied a particularly powerful space in Progressive middle-class visions of the decay caused by industrialization and immigration. The loud, ongoing harangue against prostitution filled newspapers, theater productions, and lecture halls. In the process, prostitution gained widespread legitimacy as a synonym not just for inexplicable (because no language existed to explain it) sexual practice but for unorthodox behavior in general.[72] Marital sex now joined prostitution as an open site for a variety of conversations with myriad subtexts. This loaded discourse, coupled with the inclusion of cruelty into the equation, forced an explosive reevaluation of the sexual relations between men and women, whether married or not.

IV

The growing intersection between personal behavior and public disclosure, accelerated by rising divorce rates and the Progressive Era fascination with vice, helped reorient the nature of public reference. In the search for the roots of modern sensibilities, one must pay particular attention to the discourse which incorporated images of marital sexuality. The home of appropriate sexual expression proved to be not a bastion of middle-class moral order but instead a complex, multifaceted center of sexual reconceptualization.

Early films reached into this middle-class home to produce images that contradicted the complexity of real life. The world had become too unsettling, the site of traditional order too disrupted, to allow for realistic depictions. The films, like people in the "real" world, did their best to structure these themes so that they made sense. In the movies, women were cruel, and female cruelty meant asexuality. Men were the victims of this cruelty and wished to leave their marriages. All these images had at least some grounding in the true experiences related in divorce trials. In those divorces, however, much of the cinematic text lay in shreds, and no final meaning could be derived from the testimony of sexual chaos. In the movies, masculine dominance could be restored with simplicity; many must have wished that offscreen marital issues could be so easily tamed.

If the language of real life marriage was unsettled, it stood side by side with the other sexual renegotiations discussed in this study. These fascinating conversations occurred in the everyday lives of the most uninteresting and anonymous people and in the face of a dominant moral theology reflected in the courts. Unlike most parties to sex-crime trials, whose behavior represented identified forms of "deviancy," those filing divorces came into public scrutiny as "normal" men and women. Through their testimony, they redefined that word as well as marriage itself. The public presentation of sexual codes enacted and lived out in relationships that "failed" had a profound impact on the nature of marriage. The clarity of the middle-class rhetoric on marital relations disappeared in an onslaught of extraordinarily tangled truths at the turn of the century. Despite the best efforts of many, the imperatives of marital sexuality remained forever altered.

Chapter Five

The Soubrette's Slide

When warring couples resorted to the language of prostitution in turn-of-the-century America, they stood in excellent company. Indeed, prostitution and the Progressive Era have marched off together arm in arm into historical immortality. Never before had the public been as overwhelmingly obsessed with vice as during the highly chatty reign of Progressive reformers. Historians of Progressive ideology seem equally fascinated with the subject and have adopted it as the flagship for the flotilla of studies on sexuality in this period.[1] Although this overattendance to a single aspect of sexuality provokes a certain impatience, it is hard not to be impressed by the emotional power prostitution carried at that time.

The most interesting thing about prostitution in the Progressive Era is its "discovery." Like Louie in *Casablanca*, urban reformers were "shocked, shocked" to find such goings-on in their communities. Clearly, the problem must have been new—for how could it have escaped detection? The prostitution debate centered on the rapid expansion of vice, the "enslaving" of innocents, and the degradation of urban America. The Progressives' interest in prostitution has become mythologized as but one more example of middle-class anxiety, the last gasp of Victorian prudery. Although this analysis is not incorrect, it is incomplete. When viewed in the context of the shifting sexual sensibilities documented in this study, the assault on prostitution stands as but one shout among many in the cacophonous debate over sexuality in early-twentieth-century America.

I

The discussion of prostitution stands out in this period because it was so direct. In this it differs from the other topics in this study, just as it differed from other issues of its time. In discussions of prostitution, sexuality had to be confronted directly. The subject could not be avoided or addressed in coded language as it was, for example, in the anxiety over divorce. Those concerned about rampant marital dissolution could weep for the children or rail against loss of social stability, ignoring the subject of sex altogether. Not so with antiprostitution crusaders.

Suddenly a large number of individuals had an arena in which to speak freely about the most minute detail of sexual behavior. There emerged a surprisingly extensive debate over what constituted appropriate sexual activity. Whereas concerns about gender and sexual practice or the investment of sexuality into female identity often worked on a largely subtextual level, no subtlety was employed in the harangue against prostitution. One could address sexuality openly yet deflect it away from both speakers and listeners and onto the prostitute—an obviously marginalized individual. Prostitution thus became the easiest and most available site onto which those concerns could be displaced and made less threatening.

Campaigns against prostitution provided an opportunity for people to explore questions of heterosexual practice and expectation. Although sexuality had begun to emerge as a center of personal identity, the language for that concept did not yet exist—except within the rhetoric of vice and prostitution.[2] Consequently, this discussion became a testing ground for new sexual definitions that would have enormous impact on modern sexuality.

Early filmmakers utilized images of prostitution both to mirror older understandings of sexuality and to generate new ones. These representations sprang initially from the traditional notion of prostitution as the business of selling female bodies for male sexual gratification. Moreover, early film was itself a form of "selling" bodies—for the price of a ticket, one had access to the onscreen image. Actresses became, in effect, stand-in prostitutes. By depicting burlesque queens as they stripped, barely clothed soubrettes mocking vice reformers, and, finally, middle-class women in various states of revealing dishabille, filmmakers helped introduce the idea that bodies—in this case, filmed ones—could be purchased in the service of sexual arousal. These films did not constitute pornography—although a pornographic market did exist—but they enabled sexual imagery to come out of the closet and help shape the public sensibility. Although filmmakers firmly rooted their imagery in long-standing visions of prostitution, they reoriented the audience to a new sexual coda that integrated the buying and selling of desire into normative public heterosexuality.

In these representations, prostitution ceased to function as an individual economic enterprise and became instead the underpinning for a broad-based sexual ideology. Early film used the language of sexual transaction to reorder the nature of public sexual interaction. These filmmakers provided a vision that called for the mass ownership of women's bodies, offering equal title to all who watched. In essence, they engaged not in prostitution but in the sexual colonization of onscreen bodies, with prostitution serving as both metaphor and model. To the filmmakers who produced such work, the primary topic was not prostitution or vice but rather how male desire and sexual expression were to be constructed in modern society.

Yet the intentions of those filmmakers proved irrelevant. With the advent of male screen idols such as Rudolf Valentino and Douglas Fairbanks, the sexual economy of cinema expanded to include both female heterosexual desire and male homosexual desire. Ultimately, sexual control of onscreen bodies became completely free-floating and passed into the psyches of audiences, where it continues to dwell. In the end it is impossible to claim that heterosexual male desire constitutes the dominant cinematic focus, yet as one looks at very early film, it seems quite clear that the initial deployment of prostitution imagery had an enormous impact not only on the development of cinematic tropes but on the construction of commercialized public sexuality as a whole.

This model for sexual commodification drifted from the world of prostitution into the mainstream culture through reform activities as well. When Progressive reformers initiated their judicial attack on

vice, they helped bring about extensive documentation of sexual activity that became increasingly difficult to label. Police and prosecutors, faced with behavior that defied categorization, simply had no
language, other than that of prostitution, by which to describe what
they encountered. When young women such as Almary Jones exhibited a sexual ethic that incorporated both personal autonomy and
commercial exchange, their actions could be best understood and socially contained within the rubric of prostitution.[3]

The rigidification of class lines in an industrializing society helped
both to increase the number of prostitutes and to cement their identity and status. Antiprostitution reformers in late-nineteenth-century
England and America expanded the activity's definition, "capturing"
many working-class women who drifted in and out of commercial
sexual activity in order to provide supplemental income. In the
emerging middle-class moral order, such casual movement was no
longer to be permitted. Women thus caught were marginalized. By
the time of the Progressive assault prior to World War I, reformers
had little doubt about just how a prostitute was defined. A woman engaging in prostitution was a prostitute. Why she had "fallen" might be
a subject for debate, and certainly the likelihood of her redemption
remained in dispute, but the fact of her disgrace stood secure.[4]

Yet the behavior to which many women and men of the period testified suggests that these rigid Progressive definitions may not have
truly taken hold outside of reformer discourse. Historians have uncovered a highly commercial world of sexual relations in urban
America that stood untouched by reform ideology.[5] Men and women
in big cities often exchanged sexual favors for the pleasures of social
company. As Almary Jones's Sacramento testimony showed, a similar
coda existed in rural areas and small towns. It is unclear whether this
was a new sensibility or a traditional one suddenly revealed by the
microscope of Progressive obsession. That distinction is not particularly relevant in assessing the explosive effects of the collision between reformer ideology and the now-highlighted sexual activity.

That ideology inadvertently helped reinforce new definitions of
sexuality based upon commodification. By attempting (ultimately,
with little success) to equate prostitution with certain kinds of autonomous sexual behavior, reformers inscribed commercialized sexu-

ality onto normative expressions of heterosexual desire. Although the subject was publicly visible heterosexual practice, the discourse remained rooted in the language of prostitution and sexual transaction. Consequently, the "modern" vision of public heterosexuality inevitably became infused with commercial assumptions from the start.

The deployment of prostitution as a cinematic device and its parallel use as a descriptive category for a wide range of behaviors reflect a genuine social disjuncture. Movies offered playful renderings designed to tease the audience with commodified screen images and public expressions of sexual desire. The language of the courts indicated serious befuddlement, a morass of conflicting definitions and muddy conclusions. Yet both of these very divergent sets of representations relied upon prostitution to communicate their meanings *and* their confusion. Ultimately, they produced surprisingly similar effects.

II

Early filmmakers often reached into their own ranks to bring forth a countervision to reformer images of sexual vice. Wittily mocking a dying middle-class critique against entertainers, filmmakers portrayed women engaged in vaudeville and film as fitting into some nether category of disrepute—one often under direct assault from reformers. Located in a variety of settings and presented to audiences across a wide spectrum, these films challenged their viewers to see something different in the traditional images.

Filmmakers used a remarkable diversity of approaches to portray women of "poor character." Although such women were supposed to be viewed as prostitutes, these films presented prostitution in an old way for a new reason. The word "prostitute" never appeared; indeed, it could be argued that early films refrained from showing "actual" prostitutes. Instead, early moviemakers satirized reform themes concerning "loose" women and tied them into specific antireform activities, thus clueing in their audiences to the real subject.

For example, the quasi-illicit burlesque performer appeared often in such films as a surrogate for the prostitute. Middle-class reformers who took aim at popular theater held burlesque in particular disrepute. Bawdy jokes and barely clothed women remained established staples of this genre. Burlesque crudely presented women as sexual objects and participants and had done so for many years by the time vaudeville began to rise in the late nineteenth century. It was this vision that operators such as Albee, Keith, and Pastor insisted they were trying to eliminate from the vaudeville stage. Yet this imagery did carry over from burlesque to vaudeville, despite claims to the contrary. The continuous attempts to reform vaudeville from within and the almost nonstop disclaimers that certain behaviors or types of performances would "no longer" be tolerated are but two indications that the "problem" of lewd performances remained alive throughout the period. Although official histories of burlesque tend to take theater owners at their word, in fact the line between vaudeville acts and burlesque style was often very blurry, particularly on the small-time circuits.[6]

Women of burlesque emerged as an aggressive sexual presence in early film. These women did not offer an equal exchange of passion. Their sexuality was self-contained and entirely independent of men. They were sirens encouraging male lust but disinterested in either the gaze surveying them or the results produced. This image matches closely a favorite representation of "hardened" prostitutes who cared little for those around them.[7] The burlesque queens of the early movies stood in for those prostitutes with no trouble.

The short film "From Show Girl to Burlesque Queen,"[8] produced in 1903 by A. E. Weed for American Mutascope and Biograph, provides a spectrum along which films—and, most likely, the public as well—placed wanton women. The title alone indicates a stratification; the two roles were not synonymous in at least this filmmaker's eyes. The film is essentially a striptease from a "respectable" costume to one significantly less so. As the showgirl of the title walks into a dressing room area, she begins to remove a very formidable dress. When she comes to her fourth slip, she goes behind a screen, and various items of clothing come flying over the top. Eventually she emerges dressed in a short, leotard-like outfit, brandishing a sword. A man enters the frame to admire her as the film closes.

The new burlesque queen's lack of dress and transgressive impishness indicated her sexual availability. The male observer on the screen gave the men in the audience "permission" to enjoy the illicit, unapologetic view of her body. Just as the prostitute offered her body to the paying customer, so too did the burlesque queen, both on stage and, in an important shift, on screen. Her body could be "had" for the price of admission.

Though men had been buying such privileges in burlesque houses for many years, the mass technology of cinematic reproduction fundamentally broadened the narrow commercial relationship between the burlesque performer on stage and the customer in the seat. Images of "prostitutes"—defined in the Progressive Era lexicon as women whose bodies were offered up for the purpose of sexual pleasure—began to fill the culture in a more complicated and complete way than ever before possible. As a result, the rigid categories of females available for sexual fantasy began to disintegrate under cinematic pressure. Filmmakers made clear that all women were potential participants in the emerging commercial sexual economy. The change the showgirl underwent helped enlighten the male audience with this new understanding. Anyone could move from boring respectability to delightful disrepute. Or, even more interesting, underneath the most respectable petticoats might lie the tantalizing sexuality of a burlesque queen.

The films toyed with negative stereotypes of the theater. The showgirl already occupied a kind of transitive category, neither prostitute nor paragon in turn-of-the-century culture. Yet the theater had gained a more widespread acceptance in the popular mind at this time. Actress and showgirl began to be attractive career choices for young women. Many saw such work as a way out of poverty, a reach toward propriety. Thus, even as it reinforced the Victorian mythology that all women in the theater could be compared to prostitutes, film also, coming on the heels of growing social acceptability for theatrical performers, undercut the idea of a "safe" respectability. As the layer of petticoats, with its middle-class protective gauze, was removed, a burlesque queen emerged. The reformers saw prostitutes everywhere; filmmakers, in their own way, agreed.

Cameraman Weed repeated this theme in "Troubles of a Manager of a Burlesque Show," released in 1904, also by AM&B.[9] Three women enter a theater manager's office in perfectly appropriate street attire. After he hands them skimpy leotards, the first woman, presented as large and unattractive, throws the costume at him in a huff and storms out. The other two women, presented as more conventionally appealing, emerge in short frilly outfits. The manager immediately makes a pass at one. They enact the soon-to-be-traditional chase around the desk, after which one tosses a pot of ink at him. The film ends as she huddles with the other girl while the manager mournfully blots his shirt.

The transformation of the "respectable" auditioners reminded the audience that outside appearances did not determine true identity and that such respectability was subject to remarkable flexibility. The first woman rejected sexuality when she refused the revealing costume; moreover, a burlesque queen needed to be an obtainable body reflecting certain standards of male desire. As in the old maid films, the willful asexuality of the "unattractive" female is mocked here in what is presented as ridiculous behavior. The other two women, more "appropriate" focus points for male sexual attention, immediately are subject to it as the manager assaults them. The women win the day but do not leave the scene. This image is consistent with the representation of the prostitute as one who controls sexual access and of the man as a buffoon, helpless against the power of female sexuality. These common themes, which governed many images of the tough prostitute, played well in the comedy of this era, and their growing interconnection with images of "respectable" women strongly suggests that very early cinema had a vital role in transgressing and reshaping such social boundaries.

Filmmakers also used the more complicated image of the soubrette to help blur social categories. Though any young woman in the theater could theoretically be called a soubrette, not all soubrettes worked in burlesque; it was perfectly possible to be a soubrette with the blessing of one's mother. A soubrette was "a frivolous young woman in comedies," "an actress who plays such a part," or "a soprano who sings supporting roles in comic opera."[10] No character assault was attached to the term. Yet early filmmakers often used the soubrette character to play out fantasies of female sexual aggressiveness. The soubrette and the burlesque queen became interchangeable figures on screen despite the well-established difference between the two in the real world. Through this twinning of female stage figures, the filmmakers complicated the attempt to sort women within a hierarchy of acceptability. They teased the public with a reformer-conscious vision of omnipresent immorality permeating all female entertainers, simultaneously stripping away the notion of "safe" categories.

From "A Soubrette's Troubles on a Fifth Avenue Stage" to "The Soubrette's Slide" and "The Sleepy Soubrette,"[11] all issued between 1901 and 1905, the soubrette character held a special place in early film iconography. In all these films, young women engage in activity designed to force exposure. In "A Soubrette's Troubles," a well-dressed young woman refuses male assistance and exposes herself as she climbs down from a carriage. In "The Sleepy Soubrette," the young woman's female friends lift up her blanket while she sleeps, revealing her lower body. Other films added to the "peep show" quality with their own expanded imagery. "Soubrettes in a Bachelor's Flat," released in 1903, makes a direct connection to images of vice.[12] Here, three (seemingly a magic number in these films) women in various states of undress drink and fool around with a young rake. A friend comes by to warn him that the police are coming. The three women go behind a screen and emerge in Salvation Army outfits. When the policeman enters, the four are having a prayer meeting. After the officer leaves, they celebrate.

The film's setting in a private apartment—most such romps were set in theater dressing rooms—and the explicit assumptions in operation make this an evocative example of the genre. No other early film matched "Soubrettes in a Bachelor's Flat" for the sheer audacity of its male fantasy. The presence of three undressed women in this fellow's apartment clearly signaled a sexual scene with a surprisingly rich texture. The connection to prostitution is made pointedly by the arrival of police, but it needed no such direct reference. A 1903 audience would have been incapable of missing the implication. And the play on religious reformers as an "out" for the immoral quartet made fun of the Progressives' attack on vice.

Although most soubrette characters appeared in risqué comedies, some surfaced in moralistic tales. In melodramatic fables such as "The Unfaithful Wife" (1903) and "The Downward Path" (1902),[13] the wife or daughter's fall from grace inevitably seems to involve a new occupation requiring dancing shoes. These longer movies had titled chapters to help the audience keep track of the action. In "The Downward Path," the chapter entitled "The Girl Who Went Astray" was followed by one called "The New Soubrette."[14]

Filmmakers expanded the ground for "seeing" prostitution by reaching into a safe category of entertainer and making it a playground for sexual exploration. Despite the fairly benign connotations of the word "soubrette," filmmakers did their utmost to use onscreen soubrettes as stand-in prostitutes. As with the burlesque dancer, this character's sexual activities served as a substitute for actual prostitution, simultaneously relying upon and undercutting the middle-class stereotype of entertainers. Attacks on middle-class ideology and reformers cemented these connections further. Several films placed their protagonists in open conflict with the reform movement. Clearly marking the enemy as the same, whether the subject be prostitution or burlesque, the filmmakers expanded the social identification between the two. Prostitution and its onscreen substitutes became inextricably intertwined.

"The Gerry Society's Mistake" and "The Chorus Girls and the Salvation Army Lassie"[15] presented undressed female bodies and mocked social attempts to reclothe them. The Gerry Society worked in New York City to keep underage women off the stage. Despite its limited mandate, the society operated within the essence of Progressive reform philosophy, which regarded the theater as a breeding ground for vice. "The Gerry Society's Mistake" assaulted several reform assumptions. Set in a dressing room, the film portrays four dancers in progressively greater states of dishabille. A proper-looking gentleman comes in with a policeman and attempts to have the women arrested. The women appear to show or give the gentleman something, and he leaves, whereupon they laugh and celebrate. The officer seems to know the women—they joke with him while the Gerry Society representative is there, and he joins them in their hilarity when the man leaves.

Though it is unclear precisely how the women have gotten rid of the gentleman, their reaction leaves no doubt that they have put something over on him. Making fools out of reformers was a standard pastime for popular-culture critics, and this film reinforced the "pointlessness" of the Progressive mission. These women hardly needed protection. By undressing them throughout the proceeding, the filmmaker offers more than adequate justification for reformer intervention, but he undercuts reform assumptions about underage performers by focusing upon their autonomy and their mastery of the situation. The "mistake" of the title refers not only to whatever trick the women pull on the Gerry Society official but also to the society's attempts to "rescue" such women. Though there may have been innocence somewhere for the Gerry Society to protect, it clearly was not here.

In this film, the policeman demonstrated appropriate male behavior in the procurement of these cinematic female figures. Friendly with the women, he enjoys their sexual accessibility and shares in their delight when the Gerry Society dupe leaves. Conversely, the actions of the reformer (and by extension all such male reformers) are perverse and improper. He not only attempts to intercede between the women and their audience but also fails to "see" the women in their state of undress. He thus reveals his own incapacity and is stripped of male power.

"The Chorus Girls and the Salvation Army Lassie" sounded a similar theme, with an important switch. Instead of outwitting a hypocritical, impotent male, three women confront their cultural antithesis—the virginal female reformer. In this 1903 film, three chorus girls sitting around in their dressing room in robes engage in "disreputable" activities such as drinking and smoking. One goes to answer the door, and a young woman from the Salvation Army comes in with the clear goal of saving them. They ignore her and grimace toward the camera while she makes her exhortations. The film climaxes with the women throwing off their robes to reveal various states of undress as the Salvation Army lassie flees in terror.

This satire identifies the reform movement as antisexual. The chorus girls, specific icons of sexual objectification, counterbalance the nonsexual "good girl." The chorus girls entice the audience with their sexuality, the very same attribute that challenges the young Salvation Army worker. Their disrobing, the act that makes their bodies obtainable by the audience, forces the Salvation Army lassie to confront her own body, her own sexuality. Like the movement she represents, she is threatened by this confrontation, and she runs in its face.

Such films reveal the true subtext of these cinematic characters. Officially "only" burlesque or chorus dancers, these women possessed a wanton quality reserved for prostitutes in reform ideology. As they came to stand in for prostitutes in screen lexicon, these figures became equivalent with the idea of sexuality itself. Such films provided familiar iconography and helped propel the vigorous discourse addressing sexual meaning at the turn of the century into an even larger arena of social behavior.

This larger arena was well populated by the important but often ignored peep show. The "peeps" were designed initially for individual viewing in arcades and sites of male-only entertainment, but they ultimately found a broader audience, and homosocial boundaries often broke down.[16] These films, which cast leering glances at undressing women, have often been viewed as "naughty, but nice."[17] Such dismissal is in line with the bemused attitude late-twentieth-century sophisticates sometimes hold toward the "shocking" qualities of a "glimpse of stocking," but it is unwise to regard these films with condescension. Peep shows took audiences one step further in their capacity to own onscreen bodies. They acted as a bridge between the private pornography of the nineteenth century and the public world of cinema. A large number of these films depicted men watching women undress. Though some utilized the expected theatrical setting,[18] others depicted women in everyday walks of life. In such films, middle-class women disrobe and are witnessed, or on occasion are taken advantage of, in vulnerable situations, which are played for the comedy of the stolen "peep." The voyeurism of the spectator viewing the film replicates the voyeuristic scenario depicted on screen.

Two 1903 films by A. E. Weed, "At the Dressmaker's" and "The Dressmaker's Accident,"[19] exemplify the genre. In the first film, a woman comes into a shop and removes her outer garments in order to be fitted with a corset. A male passerby enters and sees her. She hides, and he is thrown out. In "The Dressmaker's Accident," a female customer enters the shop and trips over a stool. Other women working in the shop carry her to a chair and lift her skirts to tend to her wound. This scenario is reminiscent of "The Sleepy Soubrette" and places responsibility for the unveiling on other women.

Weed was at work again in two films released on February 11, 1904. "The Way to Sell Corsets" and "A Busy Day for the Corset Models" both get quickly to the point.[20] "A Busy Day" simply has women trying on corsets for the camera, but "The Way to Sell Corsets" is more intriguing. In this film, two men enter a corset shop and look around. A male clerk comes in to assist them, and a well-dressed young woman climbs onto a platform to be fitted. While the customers watch, the clerk manipulates her body freely and begins to remove her clothing. As the salesman reaches the last of her under-clothing, he removes her head and neck, to the visible shock of the two customers, then pulls off all her clothes, revealing that she is a wire dummy. This clever use of trick editing not only helped fulfill the male fantasy of complete revelation but reinforced the objectification of female bodies.

This manual manipulation of female bodies continued in "One Way of Taking a Girl's Picture," also released in 1904.[21] A respectable woman arrives at a photographer's studio, and he helps take her dress down so that her back is fully naked. She holds the dress to cover her breasts while he positions the cloth and her upper body. A close-up of her bare back and shoulders with a facial profile closes the film.

"Peepers" in such 1905 shorts as "On the Beach at Brighton" and "The Boarding House Bathroom"[22] stand in for the theater audience. In both films, men work to get a look at naked women taking show-ers. The audience is treated to whatever the male protagonists are permitted to see; in both movies, the peepers are caught and get buckets of cold water poured on them. Countless films of this ilk were made; they contain the images for which early film is most fa-mous. As cinema historians look to "The Great Train Robbery" as the first "real" movie because of its use of plot, historians of sexuality can regard peep shows as the first salvo in the mass representation of sex-uality and female bodies. Although these films eventually disap-peared in the assault upon film "immorality," they dominated the first ten years of film production.[23]

Peep shows were outrageous precisely because they transgressed social categories. Images of middle-class women accidentally seen without clothing, intentionally spied upon, and willfully undressed by unrelated men placed them in the same general category as prostitutes who sold sexuality for male pleasure. The intent may have differed, but identical results ensued. Furious reformers recognized correctly the degree to which social boundaries would be shattered if all women were presented as and identified with those who intentionally made their bodies available to possession. Films dealing with theater performers intentionally blurred the definition of prostitution in order to speak more broadly about sexual desire; peep shows took that fuzziness one step further and threw the possibility of sexual acquisition onto any woman.

III

Whereas image makers cleverly played upon familiar sights in order to undercut moral codes and reorient the dialogue on sexual expression, those in civic authority used the language of prostitution to fill a void between the world they perceived and the values they understood. As they did so, these upholders of community virtue, no less than the filmmakers, helped redefine the terms used to describe contemporary sexual behavior, ultimately altering the way in which sexuality was understood in America.

The confusion of those attacking vice appeared regularly in trials of men charged with sex crimes related to prostitution. Women engaged in activities that seemed only comprehensible in the context of prostitution often provided evidence that aided conviction. Yet the behavior to which these women testified could only be pressed into the mold of prostitution with torturous effort. Those efforts sometimes constituted the bulk of the transcript—the behavior of the defendant often seemed less at issue than the activities of the "victim," whose conduct lay at the heart of the struggle over sexual definition.

In towns like Sacramento, no one was arrested for prostitution— only vagrancy.[24] Women arrested for vagrancy in California at the turn of the century found themselves in police court. This lower tribunal, replaced eventually by the municipal court system, dispensed justice quickly. The court meted out light punishment: offenders typically were ordered out of town, given thirty days in county jail, or often just released with a warning. Conversely, men often faced harsh penalties for consorting with prostitutes. In 1911 Progressive reformers pushed through a new law against pandering. Grand jury transcripts offer detailed testimony against men who worked with prostitutes or had unconventional sexual relationships with women.

An extraordinary level of detail appears in these accounts. Although no discussions of immunity exist in the record, it is clear by their willingness to share the intimate facts of their lives that these women had no fear of prosecution. Most of these women were in their late teens, meaning they could not be tried and punished as adults. Others undoubtedly realized that the law, though it despised them, simply had no response to their actions. Nonetheless, although these women were not officially in the dock, their testimony underscores the fact that theirs was the behavior that was truly on trial.

These accounts are complicated because so many traditional images of prostitution recur. Indeed, some *are* simply cases of prostitution. But the issue here is the degree of subtlety present not only in the participants' descriptions of their behavior but also in the questions asked and the interpretations offered by the community. The courts solicited testimony both from self-defined prostitutes and from those who did not identify themselves as such. Sometimes witnesses from each camp appeared as the court tried to carve out a set of definitions that could hold up under scrutiny. The transcripts convey the exasperated sense of confusion in the court. Even cases involving clearly marked prostitutes provoke more ambiguity than they resolve.

"Along about the twelfth of August, 1913, there came to Sacramento Maud Ellis, also known as Fay Clifford, and Annie Richard, two young girls from Fort Bragg, Mendocino County, who had left their homes with the intention of entering upon a life of ill fame."[25] So begins the almost poetic opening to the transcript of the preliminary investigation into the case against Greek immigrant Nick Dandes and six friends. All were charged with contributing to the dependency of a minor child, Maud Ellis. She and Annie Richard came from a remarkably slow small town for the kind of fast action in which they were about to engage. Fort Bragg, a tiny, isolated logging community even today, epitomized the sleepy hamlet of yesteryear. Yet eighteen-year-old Maud and seventeen-year-old Annie somehow got the notion to travel to other small communities in order to pick up cash and goods in exchange for sex. The two girls left Fort Bragg on July 10, 1913, and traveled to Willits, a virtual speck on the northern California map, where they stayed three or four days. They returned to Fort Bragg but shortly thereafter revisited Willits for a fortnight and set up shop. From here they moved on to Ukiah, another inconsequential logging village, for a week, then took off for the big city, San Francisco. Several days later the two headed east to Sacramento, stopping in Stockton long enough to get information on their destination from a waiter at a restaurant. Only after several active days in Sacramento did their California tour come to an abrupt end.[26]

Ellis and Richard made little pretense as to the nature of their actions. Indeed, their honesty makes their complex story more credible. Maud and Annie did not travel down the California coast simply plying a trade. In fact, Ellis denied any sexual activity on the first visit to Willits but hesitated not at all in admitting to her financial success the second time around. After acknowledging that their activities in Willits were "the same as we was doing in Sacramento," Ellis responded to the defense attorney's attempts to track their movements.

> Q: You stayed with a good many men there in Willits, did you not?
>
> A: Oh, no, not so many.
>
> Mr. Brown: We object to that as incompetent, immaterial and irrelevant;
> [Prosecutor]   he has established the act, and it does not make any difference whether it was one or a dozen. [Objection was overruled.]
>
> Q: Well, of course, I mean, by not a great many—but all that you could find; in other words, you hunted the men in order to do business, didn't you?
>
> A: No, I didn't hunt them.
>
> Q: Well, you were looking after doing business, weren't you, Miss Ellis; that's what you were there for, wasn't it?
>
> A: Yes sir. . . .
>
> Q: And what were you doing in Ukiah—the same thing, weren't you?
>
> A: No sir.
>
> Q: Why?

A: I didn't have to.

Q: You didn't have to. You mean that you had made money enough in Willits, and you didn't need the money there; is that it?

A: Yes sir.[27]

The young women rested up, in apparent quietude, for more than a week before moving on to San Francisco. Ellis claimed she did not engage in sexual activity in San Francisco either. Although this statement may have been disingenuous, an attempt to avoid prosecution, the women may have been out of their league. Their departure only two or three days later would suggest the likelihood that smaller towns were more their speed.

The mechanics of this kind of sexually financed travel become clear through the testimony. The waiter in Stockton urged the two young women to go to the Eagle Restaurant when they got to Sacramento and to look up his buddy, Nick Dandes. Ellis carefully addressed this conversation. Although confessing that she had told this waiter (whose name and restaurant she could not seem to recall) her business, she insisted that she had not told him that they were planning to conduct that enterprise in Sacramento. Understandably confused, the attorney pushed her somewhat on this point.

Q: Now, did you tell this waiter in Stockton what your business was— what you were doing?

A: Yes sir, we did.

Q: In other words, you told him you were rustling, did you?

A: Yes sir.

Q: And you told him you were going to Sacramento to rustle?

A: No sir; didn't say we were coming to Sacramento to rustle . . .

Q: And so that we will not misunderstand each other, I will say that I mean by rustling—that is, that you seek men to have intercourse with you, to have them pay for it; that is correct, isn't it?

A: Yes sir.[28]

Ellis staunchly maintained that neither she nor the anonymous waiter ever discussed her "rustling" in Sacramento. It seems likely that she was protecting the waiter from prosecution. He would have been subject to a pandering charge if any proof existed that a discussion of future prostitution activities in Sacramento had occurred.

No mention was made of how the travelers found the Stockton restaurant, but one can infer that they got a tip from a similar establishment in San Francisco. The ease with which Ellis and Richard made their connections suggests the existence of a reasonably well-established circuit for women wishing to engage in rustling throughout small town California. The fact that Ellis continued to protect her Stockton contact indicates either that she planned to use him again or wanted to avoid getting a reputation as an informer.

Ellis and Richard took the advice of the Stockton waiter and found Nick Dandes. Dandes "sort of guessed"[29] what the women did, even though Ellis denied telling him. Dandes recommended they get rooms at the Minerva Hotel, run by another one of the defendants, George Agyros. Ellis testified that she and Richard requested work as chambermaids from Agyros, but the defense attorney would have none of it. "Well now, wasn't the reason for telling him you wanted work as a chambermaid, a sort of bluff, to put him off, so you could get in there and get a room?" demanded Dandes's counsel.[30] Ellis insisted she would have done chamberwork if Agyros had really hired her for that. Defense counsel jeered sarcastically: "Had you made up your mind that you were going to quit rustling today, and wouldn't do any more rustling, but do work as a chamber maid?" Finally riled, Ellis snapped back: "Well, I had to have money; I couldn't starve, and I couldn't get no job."[31]

Maud Ellis's career in Sacramento was one of mixed success. Agyros had intercourse with her that first night but offered her no payment. Dandes also had sex with her on the promise of silk stockings, but he provided none, and she refused to consort with him again. Denying that she picked men up off the street, Ellis revealed that she would go to coffeehouses to "see Annie"[32] and find men, who somehow knew to follow her back to her room. One by one, the defendants rose in the courtroom to be identified as she attempted to remember them, what they had paid, and the frequency of their encounters. James Papas met her in the halls of the Minerva and paid $1.50.[33] Ellis testified that she and Annie utilized another rooming house as well, renting by the day. She described how "we would go in there and give them fifty cents for the room, and call for it as soon as we wanted during the day."[34] Defendant Nick Zotas lived there and visited her twice. More generous than the numerous other Nicks who seemed to populate this case (at least three of the defendants and one unindicted participant were named Nick), Zotas paid a dollar more than the others. Ellis described their exchange: "Well, when I left him, he says: 'How much do I owe you?' . . . And I says 'Five dollars, I guess,' and I kind of laughed, and he says 'Well, here is two and a half.'"[35]

In an angry final exchange with Maud, the defense counsel tried to gauge the extent of her work.

Q: How many men, all together, during the time you were in the city of Sacramento, stayed with you?

A: I don't know. I couldn't tell you.

Q: I want to get a guess.

A: I haven't the least idea.

Q: A hundred?

A: Oh, no. Not a hundred.

Q: Fifty?

A: No.

Q: Now, don't you think there were about fifty?

A: No sir.

Q: Well, forty?

A: No, it wasn't that many.

Q: Thirty?

A: About a dozen.

Q: About a dozen?

A: Yes sir.

Q: You mean, look here Miss Ellis—you mean there are only five others besides these seven who stayed with you in this city?

A: Yes sir.

Q: Now you do not mean that, do you?

A: Yes sir.

Admonished to stop harassing the witness, the attorney made a caustic remark about the prosecutor's generosity to Ellis and found himself in contempt of court.[36]

Defense counsel attempted, with mixed success, to bring the charge of contributing to the dependency of a minor under ridicule. By putting Ellis's and Richard's actions over a six-week period under close scrutiny, he wanted to demonstrate that his clients were not, to quote the words of the charge, steering these women toward an "idle, dissolute and immoral life." His argument certainly seems to have been reasonable. Nevertheless, the seven were bound over for trial and the prosecution struck a deal. In return for guilty pleas, each received a year's probation. Their probation orders included the insistence that each "eschew the association and company of lewd men and women or men and women addicted to fast living."[37] The ultimately sympathetic court obviously saw Annie and Maud as precisely such "addicted" women.

Traditional notions of prostitution do not apply to the traveling pair. It is not clear that they thought of themselves as prostitutes in any standard sense of the word. Sex enabled them to finance free time and pay for lodgings on their trip. Ellis's comments on the stand indicate that she viewed rustling as one of several commercial possibilities. The "vacation" set up by the two women may seem somewhat unusual, but the ease with which they planned and executed their travels indicates that they did not make up the idea themselves. Young men often set off in search of migratory work, and the existence of a female equivalent suggests that our understanding of gender-based occupational activity is somewhat incomplete for this period.

The testimony points to the presence of an established network of agents who helped route women to appropriate destinations in each community. There seems little doubt that as they shuffled from locale to locale, Richard and Ellis were directed by individuals based in rooming houses and restaurants throughout northern California. In this part of the state, one could easily make a career moving between logging and mining camps. Stockton, a feeder to the highly lucrative Sacramento market, was itself a cow town—literally. As a center for cattle auctions, Stockton became a transfer point for a variety of transactions. Though Annie and Maud did not remain longer than a half hour, it is not surprising that they stopped off there to pick up key information.

This form of prostitution offered autonomy as a central attraction. The two young women did not follow the troops, but rather went where they wanted, rested at their leisure, and had the troops come to them. The defense attorney in the Dandes case wanted to depict Annie and Maud as streetwalkers who hunted men and lured them to their rooms. Maud Ellis strongly resisted this vision on the stand, constantly indicating that she did not care whether someone guessed her willingness to rustle or not, whether someone followed her or not. She insisted that she did not chase the men who came to her and that when she sat smoking cigarettes in a coffeehouse with Annie, it was not a signal to men that she would trade in sex but simply what she wanted to do. The attorney was completely incredulous, and arguments over such issues of intent fill the transcript. Yet Ellis's attitude is actually quite credible and is reflected not only in such direct testimony but in the whole manner in which she and Richard carried out their activities.

In discussing her activities, Ellis had no words at her disposal other than the existing language of prostitution. It was also the only terminology by which the court could understand her behavior. To some degree, her mixed "success" reflected the limitations of that sensibility. She may have seen her own activities as something like prostitution—she admitted to "rustling"—yet her lackadaisical approach and frequent free encounters suggest that she was hardly the professional prostitute the defense lawyers tried to make her out to be. If prostitution offered the most serviceable vocabulary for everyone, it did not reflect a wholly accurate description of the behavior exhibited by the two women.

People v. Goldsworthy, another pandering case from 1913, proved particularly vexing to those attempting to fit sexual availability into a single definitional mold. The testimony provided fascinating insight into the world of men and women who lived and worked in houses of prostitution as well as the world of women like Maud and Annie, whose behavior skirted the edges of that community.[38] In *Goldsworthy*, as in the Dandes case, a young woman found her sexual behavior, rather than the defendant's conduct, the actual subject on trial. "Real" prostitutes were brought in to bolster the defense and tar the putative victim, producing only greater confusion.

This 205-page preliminary hearing transcript, easily the longest in this study, examines the charge that Earl "Goldie" Goldsworthy had tried to induce nineteen-year-old Beulah Willard to enter a house of prostitution. Such a felony was understandably difficult to prove conclusively. After days of testimony, the charge was dropped to contributing to the dependency of a minor. As indicated by the Dandes trial, where the defendants entered guilty pleas despite the confessed activities of Ellis and Richard, this charge needed little support and usually led to an easy conviction.

Beulah Willard wandered to Sacramento from Coquille, Oregon, in February 1913. Unlike the Fort Bragg pair, Willard seems to have made a serious effort to find legitimate employment as a waitress. After pounding the pavement looking for work, she took a break to window-shop in downtown Sacramento and found she was being followed by two young gentlemen. One flashed a winning smile, and Miss Willard's response brought down the house at the preliminary hearing.

> *Q:* And what did you do, Miss Willard?
>
> *A:* I smiled.
>
> *Q:* In what manner did you smile?
>
> *A:* A sneer.
>
> *Q:* A sneer. And upon sneering at them, as you say you did . . .
>
> *Magistrate:* Now I will have order down there or I will clear the courtroom. I don't want any of that.[39]

Despite the lukewarm response, Goldsworthy followed Willard onto a trolley, plopped himself down next to her, and began his wooing. Telling her that he was a waiter and an actor, he promised to help her get a job. They spent the afternoon and evening together, and although highly suggestive conversations occurred, "nothing of a meretricious nature" happened, according to the court.[40] Goldsworthy laid the foundation for the conversations to come by telling Willard that he had traveled in the past with a woman as man and wife. When Willard plaintively informed him that she "would like to meet some nice girl chum," he urged her to meet Maxine, whom he described as "a very nice girl, a 'jolly' girl" who "liked to have a good time" and whom he was sure Willard would like. Maxine worked at Cherry's, a known "sporting establishment" (i.e., house of prostitution): "He told me that Cherry's was a very nice place . . . He told me that he thought I could go there to work. That it was different from most places . . . it was a better place . . . He told me I could make lots of money there."[41]

Such conversations did not deter Willard from making more dates with Goldsworthy, a fact not lost upon the court.[42] Goldsworthy's defense attorney argued that her continued acquaintanceship with the young man, despite his obsession with houses of prostitution, demonstrated Willard's own dissolute character. With an eye toward proving that allegation, the attorney went after Willard's past, casting doubt upon her true purpose in Sacramento. Willard began having intercourse with Goldsworthy a week after they met. The defense established that this was not Willard's first such relationship. Her first sexual experience had been with a Clayton Moore in Oregon. Then she had lived with a man named Scruggs for several months. In Sacramento, she had intercourse twice with Bert McKay, who decided to help her get away from Goldsworthy and bought her a ticket home. The prosecution, attempting to salvage their witness's credibility, began to object to the line of questioning: "Well, if the court please, they ask her whether or not she has had intercourse with him; she says no; I think right there the matter should cease . . . Now as far as any reference is made by counsel that she has had promiscuous intercourse, I deny it; she says three parties, thus far, and that is all they have proven."[43]

Because three parties apparently constituted insufficient proof of promiscuity, the defense attorney attempted to prove that Willard was actually a prostitute. He accused her of arranging encounters with various men, all of which she denied flatly. However, she confirmed that such an exchange had almost occurred but insisted that nothing actually transpired.

Q: Do you recall the owner of the hotel coming to you and telling you he had a man that wanted to stay with you?

A: Yes sir.

Q: And didn't you say to Goldsworthy: "I am going to meet this man; I need the money"; ain't that so?

A: But I didn't go.

Q: Wait a minute, didn't you say that to Goldsworthy?

A: Yes sir.[44]

Willard refused to concede anything more about the incident, particularly denying that Goldsworthy had paid her $2.50 not to meet
the other fellow. In the only other lapse in her forty pages of de-
nials, Willard admitted that she had told Goldsworthy of her bout
with a venereal disease but insisted that it had occurred "a long
time ago."[45] All of this information obviously encouraged the would-
be pimp in his attempts to convince Willard to enter a genuine
house of prostitution. The pair were often accompanied by
Goldsworthy's best friend, C. H. Hubbard, whose girlfriend/wife
(her actual status and even her name remain quite confused
throughout the hearing), Babe, lived in such a house in Nevada City
in the Sierra foothills. According to the defense attorney, Hubbard
and his wife were the true culprits. He demanded to know from
Beulah Willard:

> *Q:*   Didn't Hubbard tell you that you would have to have a
> medical certificate to go into a house of assignation?
>
> *A:*   Not that I remember.
>
> *Q:*   Didn't he tell you how to handle a man?
>
> *A:*   Not that I remember.
>
> *Mr. Cross:* I do not quite understand the question—how she should
> *[Prosecutor]* handle a man; that is too general.
>
> *Mr. Welch:* Well, we don't want to go into details; it is too delicate to go
> into details, we think.[46]

When Hubbard took the stand, the delicate details emerged:

Q: Didn't you tell her how to handle a penis, and show her how to do it?

A: No sir, I did not. There was no such language as that used in my
presence.[47]

Although defense counsel was unable to prove anything against
Hubbard, his world obviously intrigued the court. His testimony and
that of his cohorts about the "sporting life" filled more than a hundred pages of transcript.

Hubbard went by many names, including "Cyclone," "Racehorse,"
and the eternal "Slim."[48] He had met his wife walking her home from
her "crib" in Sacramento[49] and married her in 1911 while she worked in
a "house of ill fame in Chico."[50] The defense called Charles Pendleton,

a waiter who had known Hubbard as "Crazy Horse Myers" in Salt Lake City. When Pendleton met him, Hubbard worked in the Chesapeake Cafe, which Pendleton admitted was a sporting house—"Well, it is, yes sir, practically, according to our estimation, it was. It was a cafe, but it had boxes and everything in there." On the cross-examination, the prosecutor attempted to undercut Pendleton's testimony.

Q: You say it was a sporting house, where he was?

A: No, I say the sporting class traded there.

Q: Well, that question was asked you and you said it was a sporting house.

A: No, I say it was a cafe and according to our classification of these cafes, it was a sporting house, . . . a hookshop.

Q: A hookshop?

A: No, it was a cafe and they had their boxes and everything to cater to the sporting class of people.

Q: Did not a respectable class of people go in that place too?

A: Certainly; they always do.[51]

If the Chesapeake had been a true house of prostitution, such as the Palace in Nevada City, there would have been no confusion as to its definition. The defense, in its attempt to pin the blame on Hubbard, brought Rose Potter from the Nevada City house and tried to prove that she was the illusive Babe Norton. In another tactic, it attempted to prove that Goldsworthy's proposed destination was merely a rooming house and that Potter's activities there represented her private business.

Q: Miss Potter, I will ask you if men sleep in that house nightly?

A: A man can sleep there all night, with a woman in the house as a companion.

Q: They do sleep there?

A: With a woman in the house in her bed only.

Q: They pay the woman, do they?

A: They pay the woman for her services.

Q: And for the rent of the room?

A: No, not for the rent of the room.

Q: How do you know that?

A: Because I am the landlady.[52]

Having failed on that line of questioning, the attorney fished for other proof that the nature of the Palace might have been misunderstood by a naive Goldsworthy. He asked Potter, "What do you advertise that house up in Nevada City as?" She replied that she advertised it as a sporting house and carried her own cards to hand out when appropriate. The attorney pressed: "Is there any such wording on the cards as a house of prostitution?"

A: The price of the house is on the cards.

Q: Pardon me; I ask you to answer my question: Is there any such wording on the card as a house of assignation or a house of prostitution or anything descriptive of it—of what you say the place is.

A: I think that is descriptive when the price is put on.

Q: What is on the card?

A: The names of the ladies and the price of the house, two dollars and fifty cents.[53]

Frustrated, the magistrate took over the questioning and obtained details of operation which were probably familiar to many men of his generation. Potter told him there were five bedrooms plus a dance hall and three parlors at the Palace. Five girls, one for each bedroom, lived there and were "allowed the privilege of taking men to their rooms." Though some men came just to dance and drink, most men "come in and ask for a certain woman; others are solicited," testified the madam.

Q: And suppose a man solicited a particular women, what took place then?

A: Why, she asks him to go to the room with her.

Q: I see. How often does that take place?

A: During the month—

Q: Interrupting: During a day or night?

A: Well. I should say—there are five girls in the house, and each girl averages from five to six trips to her room.

Q: And that took place how often during the month of February?

A: Every night.

Q: Every night?

A: Yes sir.[54]

The magistrate was sympathetic toward the newest proprietor of the Palace, which had, according to testimony, been in operation more than twenty-five years: "I can't help feeling, Mr. Welch, that there has been an injustice done this witness in bringing her down here, because it seems to me that you have brought her down here simply and solely for the purpose of more punishment than anything else and I must say to you that I don't like that kind of tactic."[55] Irritated, he lessened the charge against Goldsworthy to contributing to the dependency of a minor, though he still had the defendant bound over for trial. Eventually Goldsworthy was convicted and served a year in county jail. Though not a long sentence, it indicated that the court found his solicitations of Willard more offensive to the community than the simple act of intercourse, for which the defendants in the Dandes trial received a lighter response only a few months later.

The world of prostitution described in the Goldsworthy trial represented a much more traditional vision of the profession than that presented in the Dandes trial. Interestingly, it seems to have been the established, even "old-fashioned," nature of the prostitution conducted at the Palace that led the magistrate to feel sympathetic toward its denizens. Though Goldsworthy did go to jail, he got a slap on the wrist; one suspects the sentence had more to do with the magistrate's annoyance over the defense attorney's tactics than with the "crime" itself, which never actually occurred. Goldsworthy may have tried to get Beulah Willard up to Nevada City, but she never went, and there was more than a little doubt cast upon the nature of her activities in Sacramento and before.

The prosecution's attempt to paint Beulah Willard as the innocent prey of a potential "white slaver" was suspect from the start. Indeed, the prosecutor was forced to defend Willard's virtue on the basis of "only" three lovers and one bout of venereal disease. Apparently, either Progressive Era definitions of virtue had been stretched to their limits in this case or those lines were always a bit more fuzzy than we have been led to believe. The latter possibility supports the conclusion that it was precisely the inability to identify which women were "true" prostitutes that led to community discomfort.

Though Ellis and Richard were obviously more "on trial" than Willard was, none of these women helped the court make precise statements of morality. The magistrate could be sympathetic to Rose Potter; she, at least, lived in a world he understood and whose definitional walls remained as solid as the Palace's doors. Potter was a prostitute who knew her place and stayed within it until dragged to Sacramento by a desperate attorney. Conversely, Beulah Willard traveled through California in an apparent moral fog. Cloudy as to her past or the purpose of her present, Willard showed a face of surprising innocence within the context of a fairly sordid history. While the members of the court ultimately debated her mental competence, it was Beulah Willard's complicated image of female virtue that left them just as deeply befuddled. The defense attorney tried with all his might to fit Beulah Willard into the context of prostitution. Certainly he had some superficial testimony in his favor. Here was a young woman who seemed to have sexual relations easily with men she did not know well. She accepted favors from them and appeared willing on at least one occasion to sell her services. She smiled tolerantly through days of debate over whether she should enter a house of prostitution. Surely this was indeed a prostitute. Yet in this line of argument the contrasts were drawn too sharply. A very formalized system of official prostitution stood as the model before the court and the community. The people did not prove their case against Goldsworthy, and by lowering the charge to contributing to the dependency of a minor, the magistrate agreed with the defense that Beulah Willard's character did not meet proper standards. Yet the translation from the world of Rose Potter to that of Beulah Willard was a tortured one. In Beulah Willard, the court encountered an individual for whom it simply had no adequate description.

If the language of prostitution was the only one available to describe perplexing sexual practices, it also proved useful in codifying racial fears. The use of white-slaver imagery to attack new European immigrants in the East is well documented, but communities such as Sacramento also drew connections between prostitution and the perceived problem of increased racial diversity. By locating the activities of individuals of color within the framework of vice, their presence could be explained and contained. It is not accidental that the

Chinese in California and across the country were represented extensively within the context of drug use and its attendant release of sexual inhibitions. White slavers were often portrayed as Asians.[56] The *Sacramento Bee* periodically reported on young Japanese women sold into prostitution by their evil fathers. Prostitution provided a set of meanings by which to contain sexual discomfort when faced with racial others. Such usage helped cement a modern discursive relationship between race and unacceptable sexuality.

African Americans and Asian immigrants tried to live peacefully in Sacramento.[57] The *Sacramento Bee*, an appallingly racist newspaper when it came to Japanese immigrants in the delta region, apparently saw itself as the beacon of civility on race relations between African Americans and whites. The paper regularly commented on the "long-suffering Negro race" and often celebrated "uplifting" achievements by African American educators and speakers.[58] Yet, as we shall see, this tolerance had its limits. Japanese immigrants were treated with greater cruelty, and although they constituted the largest minority group in the area, few cases involving them came before the Sacramento Superior Court. Japanese immigrants seemed determined to stay out of the way of Sacramento law enforcement. Given the anti-Japanese sentiments widely held and openly expressed by the white establishment in Sacramento, this reticence demonstrated a wise sense of caution. Though most Japanese émigrés presumably were law-abiding citizens, there were problems among them, and their underrepresentation in criminal records suggests an active strategy of avoiding the justice system. This suspicion is strengthened by the almost total absence of Japanese names in the civil courts. It may simply be that cultural differences kept Japanese immigrants from filing suits, but nothing could keep them from *being* sued except an active desire to avoid contact with a system whose racism and bias lay on the surface for all to see.

This bias and the community's difficulty in separating race from sexuality are nicely illustrated in the 1911 grand jury investigation of Yoshihei Otsu,[59] charged with permitting his wife to remain in a house of prostitution. Steeped in stereotypes and racism, the Otsu case reveals a confused grand jury whose assumptions could not even be properly expressed, let alone disentangled. The grand jury heard the tale of Otsu's tortured wife, forced at gunpoint into houses of prostitution up and down the West Coast until, desperately ill, she finally ran away to neighbors and was rescued. After the hearing, Otsu, known as a "gunfighter," paid off the police, and his case was ultimately dismissed.[60]

As testimony was taken, members of the grand jury claimed to have more than a passing familiarity with the Japanese quarter of Sacramento, continuously interrupting police testimony with their own observations. Unfortunately, they seemed completely unable to tell one marginalized community from another. In one instance, when a testifying officer identified a specific address as a residential unit in the "respectable part of the Japanese quarter," a juror jumped in to interrupt.

Q: Well, aren't there women there?

A: Not that I know of. I know there is some part of town down there where we have trouble, where there is some colored women rustling down there . . . I have had reports; but we never had reports of Japanese places down there.

Q: I thought there were some Japanese places down in that alley.

A: Not that I am aware of.

Q: Well, colored women who mix with Japanese?

A: I beg your pardon?

Q: Colored women who mix with the Japanese?

A: We have raided the places down there several times. This is not in this quarter . . . down on 3rd street where there is colored women solicits Jap trade down there . . . been after them several times; run them out; as for anything else is concerned there is nothing that I know of; there is no Japanese houses down there that I know of.[61]

The juror's confusion well stated the problem faced by people of color in communities like Sacramento. "Colored women," "the Japanese," "down in that alley," "not in this quarter"—in the eyes of many white Sacramento residents, all minority races melded into a single "other" at a certain point, and it was best left to the police to sort them out in vice raids. Otsu never did come to trial, and the lack of concern for his wife's virtue or even survival speaks volumes about the racism and hypocrisy present in Progressive reform rants about female purity.

Otsu had better luck than Romeo Brown Green, an African American arrested and charged under a pimping statute enacted by the 1911 California state legislature. He was the first Sacramento man brought up on such charges and one of the few so charged at all through World War I. Although the legislature obviously felt a burning need to prohibit men from "deriving support from the earnings" of women engaged in prostitution activity, to quote from the indictment against Green, prosecutors in Sacramento clearly did not share the sense of crisis.[62] Green was the only African American defendant identified by color in the court documents surveyed for this study. By contrast, the nationality of Japanese or Chinese defendants was routinely noted; for them, racial background not only was deemed important to state but in many cases clearly influenced the nature and/or the outcome of the charge. In targeting Green and identifying him by race, the court indicated where the line of community tolerance would be drawn. It was etched not in Green's pimping activities but in the color of the prostitute who worked for him: "Ray Vernon is a prostitute, and a street walker, apparently a white woman, having a negro, Romeo Brown Green, who generally travels under the name of Romeo Brown, for a pimp."[63]

The issue of miscegenation helps explain why Green became one of the few Sacramento men charged with pimping under the 1911 law. The fact that he lived with a white woman seems to have shocked the court sufficiently to deem racial identification necessary. The doubt about Vernon's color reinforces the transgressive quality of her relationship with Green. Her involvement with an African American not only caused the court to doubt its understanding of racial categories but also caused others to have even more widespread doubts. Prosecutors asked Al Toland, the proprietor of the hotel where the two were registered as man and wife, if he knew Vernon's occupation. He claimed ignorance and mused further that he did not even know if she was a man or a woman. To the prosecutor's somewhat shocked retort, the innkeeper repeated himself—"In fact I don't know whether she is a man or a woman, so I couldn't tell [whether she was a prostitute]; but I suppose she is."[64] The prosecutor let the matter drop, a rare demonstration of good judgment among Sacramento attorneys (who, as the cases in this book show, were notorious for asking one question too many in these matters).

Vernon's sexual advances to men of color dominated the case against her, even though she was officially charged with a nonsexual offense—grand larceny. Green and Vernon had lived together for four or five months and carried on what seems to have been a fairly lucrative streetwalking practice. According to the testimony that emerged, Vernon sought "patronage on the street and steering the men toward Howard House and to various other lodging houses in the City of Sacramento, where, for a consideration, she indulges in sexual intercourse with such men, her activities being most prominent amongst Hindus, Chinamen and negros."[65]

This kind of racial intermingling was relatively unusual. Many houses of prostitution remained racially segregated; some of the larger ones offered racial divisions by floors. As the Otsu case revealed, though interracial prostitution did occur, it could be better understood if a "colored" prostitute was involved. A white prostitute who lived with an African American man and had sex almost exclusively with men of color was thus a triple outcast.[66]

The sentencing in the Green and Vernon cases clarifies the issue that truly enraged the court. Despite the utter contempt expressed for Green's character, his sentence was surprisingly light. He pled guilty and received two years in prison. This punishment may have been the result of an earlier plea bargain, as Green testified against Vernon in the grand larceny case filed against her. Although Vernon also testified against Green in the pimping trial, the judge was not so kind to her. "Common prostitutes" rarely received more than thirty days in jail; six months was the longest sentence given to a woman for any sex crime in Sacramento during this period. Courts almost always dismissed other criminal charges against women; in the Progressive version of chivalry, judges often saw them as victims of their own weakness and male domination. They could not be held accountable. Ray Vernon, however, received no such gentle treatment. The judge made clear that her guilt on the ostensibly higher charge of grand larceny was not the factor that sent her to San Quentin for two years, an extraordinarily harsh sentence. He thundered at Vernon in explanation: "Your conduct has been, if not criminal, excessively reprehensible in other ways than the crime here charged against you."[67]

By crossing color lines in such dramatic fashion, Vernon drew the explosive rage of the judge. One has only to compare this reaction to that of the magistrate who sympathized with Rose Potter from the Palace in Nevada City to note the apoplectic difference. Vernon's sexual activity broke too many boundaries, to the point that prostitution became a minor issue. Yet once again, only the lexicon of prostitution held the possibility for descriptive containment. The judge harangued her that "it is painful to anybody to have to sentence a woman; but when a woman steps down from the pedestal of purity, where she belongs, and does what you have clearly done . . . it becomes the duty of the judge to inflict such punishment as the law provides."[68]

This familiar Progressive rhetoric represents the standard line on female purity. Its presence in this particular case, with such "excessively reprehensible" behavior, demonstrates well the limitations faced by the judge. The court's rage lay not in the fact of Vernon's prostitution but rather in the racial composition of her clientele. Vernon's crime exceeded prostitution; prostitution could barely expand to encompass it.

IV

The imagery of prostitution in the courts underwent subtle restructuring, whereas that in the popular culture witnessed a much more dramatic transformation. This is not surprising, given how much earlier the shifts in popular representations began. Though it would be simplistic to attribute the change in the courts directly to the manipulations of the popular imagery, it would be foolish to ignore the fact that the expansion in the concept of prostitution as a tool for representing sexual desire first took place in film and vaudeville. Though on the surface the legal and entertainment worlds seem to have used the term differently, both refashioned "prostitution" to facilitate a new way of understanding sexuality, and in this the two arenas matched.

Filmmakers saw in prostitution a code for reshaping the open conversation on sexuality. They called forth a particular form of sexual ownership, helping to shape the sexual desire felt by the audience and offering each viewer private title to the body on screen. By playing upon images of prostitution, both direct and implied, filmmakers helped orient a new public dialogue on sexual expression. Despite the clear emphasis on male heterosexual desire in these images, to dismiss them as only affecting men would be a disservice to their cultural power. These films publicly located sexuality in women's bodies, thereby crafting an acceptable sexual space for both men and women which profoundly influenced the development of a public sexual culture. The deployment of traditional notions of commercialized sex in order to depict a public vision of access and desire at the turn of the century demonstrates that modern commercialized sexuality has deep roots in this initial cinematic moment. In an era obsessed with "vice," people on screen stood in for sexual actors in the audience, and no one could be completely immune from the message.

It may have been precisely this concern that encouraged the police and courts to describe an incomprehensible world of racial and sexual chaos by using the terms of prostitution. Reformers on the march claimed to know what prostitution meant and saw its rise in every corner. Yet the behavior exhibited in turn-of-the-century America did not fit the rigid reformer ideology. Reaching into the only dictionary they knew, the enormously conservative Progressives spoke of prostitution because they lacked other words to describe the world around them. In doing so, they, along with the filmmakers, helped develop an entirely new understanding of public sexuality in which desire and commerce became permanently intertwined.

Conclusion

We leave our story on the eve of World War I. Sexual culture in the war years and after is a tale well told by others. We have often credited our sexual mores to the events of this later time. Yet the cultural contests that helped introduce codes of public heterosexuality into the society at large had raged for at least some twenty years before the Great War. The sexual "innovations" of postwar America were but expansions of earlier cultural footholds.

Those footholds involved the design of a public sexual culture that encouraged heterosexual men and women to proclaim their desires openly, proudly to acknowledge their sexual needs. It insisted that sexual desire should be a part of one's personal identity and that it should be visible to the community at large. In the nineteenth century, men and working-class women were permitted a visible sexual culture but one circumscribed by community disapproval and disdain. In the twentieth century, reformers tried to eradicate even this limited sexual world but were drowned out by the insistence that all white men and women, regardless of class, had the right to a public sexual identity.

The rules of this new public sexual culture promoted and confirmed a specific heterosexuality. They both contained and expanded previously accepted principles of public behavior. Only certain women and men had access to and permission for public displays of desire; those who fell outside the bounds faced ferocious consequences. Older single women, effeminate men, and people of color served as very sharp edges to the world of public heterosexuality, terrible fates to be avoided. Yet for those able and willing to stay within the boundaries, great promise awaited—sexual pleasure without regard to gender or class. The racism of these sexual texts feels tiresomely familiar, but their freewheeling appeal to white men and women of all classes helps explain their ultimate historical power.

Those producing national entertainment intentionally blurred class lines, and that cloudiness was reinforced by the mixed composition of the audience. Class did not act as the primary arbiter of these new definitions. Though reformers often sounded the alarm of working-class "degeneracy" and summoned middle-class virtue to effect a national rescue, this is precisely the discourse that appears to have been universally ignored in the development of modern sexual codes. It would be incorrect to conclude that class played *no* part in the growth of changing sexual definition. Instead, as popular entertainment brought sexuality into the dominant culture, traditional assumptions about class and sexuality were specifically removed so that sexuality could be constructed as its own entity, unconnected to imperatives of class.

In communities around the country, however, class was not so easily dismissed. The power of the state in the enforcement of sexual norms fell most heavily on those working-class individuals deemed suspect by middle-class reformers. The selective nature of prosecutions cannot be ignored, but neither can the dynamic that emerged be dismissed under the rubric of simple oppression. Whatever the rationale for the assaults, the end result was an expanding public discourse on sexual practice. That discourse may originally have centered on urban working-class individuals, but inevitably it came to include middle-class men and women as well as those based in rural America. Ultimately, the Progressive attack on working-class "vice" reinforced the "classless" popular representations. With the help of both discourses, sexuality broke free from nineteenth-century class moorings and became a separate reality with its own special context.

Perhaps it was the shift away from class as a prime signifier that forced a greater emphasis on finding heterosexuality, or its absence, marked on the body itself. That marking process appeared throughout the texts surveyed in this book. In many ways it formed a running commentary on the disjuncture between the images present in popular entertainment and the often futile exhortations made by civic authorities in courts of law. The need to identify acceptable heterosexual practice appeared in both arenas, and although their intentions may appear to have been different, the outcomes proved surprisingly congruous. They helped produce the necessary syntax for the twentieth-century language of public sexuality.

These texts illustrate a productive process—something fresh emerged. They not only called out a method for seeing and categorizing sexual behaviors but also called forth those very activities and helped propel different sensibilities. It was a dynamic, interactive process that created something new even as it documented something old. One sees this dual development most significantly in the way that early cinematic images recycled older sexual stereotypes to produce new, twentieth-century icons and in the haunting resistance to civic authority in the struggle over sexual meaning and morality.

The attempt to control the emerging public culture and limit it to particular visions of acceptable heterosexuality was flawed from the start. Ensnared by a troubling revolt among women empowered by their rights to sexual pleasure, early film tried to strip marriage of sexual potential. This kind of imagery, a fundamentally conservative backlash against growing female dissatisfaction in marriage, proved counterproductive. In the end, the struggle to contain marital strife undermined the idea that marriage killed desire and forced sexual satisfaction to the top of the marital agenda. Although not part of the original boundaries created in turn-of-the-century culture, marital sexuality did not contravene the heterosexual imperative. The expansion of the public sexual culture to include desire within marriage supported the overall goal.

However, those who denied heterosexuality flummoxed one and all and undercut the restriction of public culture to heterosexuals. To be sure, homosexuality already had a niche in the public space or there would have been no need to find its mark on suspect individuals. When vaudeville reviewers discussed the "offensive" attributes of certain performers, they spoke to a knowing audience; when the *Sacramento Bee* alerted its readers to homosexual activity, this was not headline news. Still, the growing concern over gender instability and the need to shape the public sexual culture drove the campaign against antiheterosexual practice. As the record shows, this did not succeed. For every man stamped with this month's visible sign, abandoned to a nongendered purgatory, and shunned as unacceptable, there arose an accommodating cultural space generated by the search. However, cultural accommodation, whether shifting or stable, does not guarantee a happy real-life outcome. Prosecutions against homosexuality accelerated, and laws against cross-dressing gained force. The pleasure that many found in impersonators such as Julian Eltinge was hounded from public view. Eltinge's sad fate is indicative. In 1940, destitute, he tried to appear at a small nightclub in Los Angeles and applied for an exemption to a new city ordinance forbidding male or female impersonation. Denied the waiver, Eltinge stood in front of a rack of clothing and described his past glory in each. The popular joys of 1912 had become the criminal perversions of 1940.

Conversely, the criminal sexuality of 1910—prostitution—served as a basis for the daily public sexual culture of 1940 and beyond. Sexuality and desire became the foremost commodities in an open market of cultural exchange. In the twentieth century, sex sells, and anyone can buy. Early-twentieth-century deployment of prostitution imagery and rhetoric to depict the everyday life of heterosexual relations helped propel the historical forces that made sex merely another consumable good.

The roots to what we know as a modern sexual culture are readily apparent in the stories contained within these pages. These tales shed light on the complex processes by which that sensibility began to be encoded into the dominant culture. In the end, the pieces to this puzzle do not create a complete picture; we never will know exactly what Charlie Harlan was thinking. But from these stories we have a much better idea of the sexual world visible to everyone surrounding him. Individually, each story is fascinating, but together they create a tapestry from which we can easily see the interwoven threads of sex and culture in turn-of-the-century America.

Notes

Chapter One. Pulling off the Bedclothes

1. Case #1866, July 18, 1899, testimony of C. L. Stanfield in the Engrossed Bill of Exceptions filed on appeal of the conviction of Charles Harlan for rape. Records of Superior Court, Criminal Division, County of Sacramento, Sacramento City Archives.

2. Michel Foucault, *The History of Sexuality*, Vol. 1, *An Introduction*, trans. Robert Hurley (New York: Pantheon, 1978).

3. See in particular Kathy Peiss, *Cheap Amusements: Working Women and Leisure in Turn of the Century New York* (Philadelphia: Temple University Press, 1986), and George Chauncey, *Gay New York: Gender, Urban Culture, and the Making of the Gay Male World (1890–1940)* (New York: Basic Books, 1994). For an excellent overview see John D'Emilio and Estelle Freedman, *Intimate Matters: A History of Sexuality in America* (New York: Harper and Row, 1988).

4. For interesting discussions of the role advertising played in the development of modern sexuality and twentieth-century gender structures, see Roland Marchand, *Advertising the American Dream: Making Way for Modernity, 1920–1940* (Berkeley: University of California Press, 1985); Richard Wightman Fox and T. J. Jackson Lears, eds., *The Culture of Consumption: Critical Essays in American History, 1880–1980* (New York: Pantheon Books, 1983); T. J. Jackson Lears, *Fables of Abundance: A Cultural History of Advertising in America* (New York: Basic Books, 1994); Ellen Gruber Garvey, *The Adman in the Parlor: Magazines and the Gendering of Consumer Culture, 1880s to 1910s* (New York: Oxford University Press, 1996); and Jennifer Scanlon, *Inarticulate Longings: The Ladies' Home Journal, Gender, and the Promises of Consumer Culture* (New York: Routledge, 1995).

5. Initially, filmmakers sent paper print copies developed from the original nitrate negatives to the Library of Congress for copyright purposes. This procedure continued until 1912, when a specific law addressing the motion-picture industry went into effect and provided for the sending of negative film. The early rolls of paper sat around in the archives rotting away until the 1950s, when restoration began; the paper prints were refilmed and essentially turned back into movies. More than 3,000 films, dating from 1894 to 1912, are part of the Paper Print Collection. The published guide to the collection is by Kemp R. Niver, *Early Motion Pictures: The Paper Print Collection in the Library of Congress* (Washington: Library of Congress, 1985).

6. Sacramento population drawn from *Twelfth Census of the United States 1900, Vol. II, Population, Part II* (Washington, D.C.: United States Census Office, 1902), 640. Sacramento, the state capital since 1854, still saw itself as and acted the part of a sleepy small town. The Sacramento economy was heavily based on regional agriculture, reinforcing the rural sensibility. I was advised by numerous Sacramento natives that this small-town feeling exists even today—though the city's population has surpassed a million.

In 1900, residents of the town proper were often employed by the Southern Pacific Railroad. Unofficial estimates place 60 to 75 percent of Sacramento workers on the SP payroll at the turn of the century. The overwhelming majority of employed individuals who surfaced in this study, both through criminal activity and divorce records, worked for the Southern Pacific Railroad. As the largest landowner in the state of California at the time, the SP likely had dealings with many farmers and farm laborers, the other major occupational category in Sacramento during this era. Sacramento is consequently an interesting community, with a varied population from which to draw information. Heavily rural, it also contained a growing working class, an established middle class, and a powerful elite whose connections to the railroad and state politics created an inevitable schism in community identity.

Census figures for 1890 indicate that 230 U.S. communities, including Sacramento, had populations of 10,000 to 25,000; 994 communities had populations between 2,500 and 10,000; 113 communities had populations between 25,000 and 250,000; and 11 cities had populations greater than 250,000. Virtually all work on sexuality at the turn of the century has been done in those eleven largest centers (*Historical Statistics of the United States, Colonial Times to 1957* [Washington D.C.: U.S. Bureau of the Census, 1961]). No scholarly study of Sacramento history has been done, although numerous popular histories focusing on the Gold Rush do exist. For other information pertaining to Sacramento, see "Sacramento: A

Chronological History," a pamphlet produced by the Sacramento History Center, Museum and History Division (January 1984). For general history of California, see Walton Bean and James Rawls, *California: An Interpretive History*, fourth edition (Berkeley: University of California Press, 1987); and Richard B. Rice, William A. Bullough, and Richard J. Orsi, *The Elusive Eden: A New History of California* (New York: Knopf, 1988).

7. See, for example, Robert Sklar, *Movie-Made America: A Social History of American Movies* (New York: Random House, 1975); Lary May, *Screening Out the Past: The Birth of Mass Culture and the Motion Picture Industry* (New York: Oxford University Press, 1980); Lester D. Friedman, ed., *Unspeakable Images: Ethnicity and the American Cinema* (Urbana: University of Illinois Press, 1991); Roy Rosenzweig, *Eight Hours for What We Will: Workers and Leisure in the Industrial City, 1870–1920* (Cambridge: Cambridge University Press, 1983); and Peiss, *Cheap Amusements*.

8. See Charles Musser, *The Emergence of Cinema: The American Scene* (Berkeley: University of California Press, 1990), for the authoritative history of this era.

9. Ibid., 122.

10. Ibid., 367.

11. Historian Edward Lowry describes the route of one such early exhibitor, Edwin J. Hadley, through 1897 and 1898. Hadley visited Warrensburg (pop. 2,267), Ticonderoga (pop. 2,000), and the big town of Glen Falls, New York (pop. 10,000), then went to the Midwest, where he appeared in Lincoln, Illinois (pop. 8,962), and Louisiana, Missouri (pop. 5,131). Lowry assumes that Hadley's stops included many for which there were no records. Edward Lowry, "Edwin J. Hadley: Traveling Film Exhibitor," in John L. Fell, ed., *Film Before Griffith* (Berkeley: University of California Press, 1983), 131–143.

12. Sklar, *Movie-Made America*, 13.

13. See particularly Robert C. Allen, *Vaudeville and Film 1895–1915: A Study in Media Interaction* (New York: Arno Press, 1980).

14. Robert C. Allen, "Contra the Chaser Theory," in Fell, *Film Before Griffith*, 105–115. Allen disputes the chaser theory, whereas Musser argues that after the initial novelty period, vaudeville patrons indeed found the films repetitive and boring. He claims that after the introduction of narrative films in 1903, vaudeville owners once again began to demand more movies. See Musser, *Emergence of Cinema*, chapters 10 and 11.

15. For a more extensive history of early film, see Musser, *Emergence of Cinema*; Charles Musser, *Before the Nickelodeon: Edwin S. Porter and the Edison Manufacturing Company* (Berkeley: University of California Press,

1991); Allen, *Vaudeville and Film*; Tino Balio, ed., *The American Film Industry* (Madison: University of Wisconsin Press, 1976); Fell, *Film Before Griffith*; May, *Screening the Past*; and Sklar, *Movie-Made America*.

16. Allen, *Vaudeville and Film*, 25–28. For further information on vaudeville, see Robert W. Snyder, *The Voice of the City: Vaudeville and Popular Culture in New York* (New York: Oxford University Press, 1989); Charles W. Stein, ed., *American Vaudeville as Seen by Its Contemporaries* (New York: Knopf, 1984); Anthony Slide, *The Vaudevillians: A Dictionary of Vaudeville Performers* (Westport: Arlington House, 1981); Robert C. Toll, *On with the Show: The First Century of Show Business in America* (New York: Oxford University Press, 1976); John DiMeglio, *Vaudeville, U.S.A.* (Bowling Green: Bowling Green University Popular Press, 1973); and Albert F. McLean, Jr., *American Vaudeville as Ritual* (Lexington: University of Kentucky Press, 1965).

17. Historian Robert Allen notes that one 1896 report identified "more than seventy-five full time vaudeville theaters, with houses in cities as small as Paducah, Kentucky, Leadville, Colorado, [and] Butte, Montana." According to Allen's data, the number of theaters increased by at least 12 percent annually through 1906, when another survey reported more than 400 such theaters. Full-time vaudeville houses represented only one type of venue for traveling acts and films. Many performers showed up in small-town "opera houses" or "legitimate" theaters, which rented out to the itinerant vaudevillians when stock drama companies were not available. In Sacramento they came to the Clunie Opera House. Such makeshift theaters were included in the equally rough estimate of legitimate theaters made in the period. Allen, *Vaudeville and Film*, 35–36. For a discussion of film exhibited at county fairs, see Mark E. Swartz, "An Overview of Cinema on the Fairgrounds," *Journal of Popular Film and Television* 15 (Fall 1987): 102–108.

18. See particularly Laura Mulvey, "Visual Pleasure and the Narrative Cinema," *Screen* 16 (Autumn 1975): 6–18; Laura Mulvey, *Visual and Other Pleasures* (Bloomington: Indiana University Press, 1989); Tom Gunning, "An Aesthetic of Astonishment: Early Film and the Incredulous Spectator," *Art and Text* 34 (1989): 31–45; Miriam Hansen, *Babel and Babylon: Spectatorship in American Silent Film* (Cambridge: Harvard University Press, 1991); Janet Staiger, *Interpreting Films: Studies in the Historical Reception of American Cinema* (Princeton: Princeton University Press, 1992); Judith Mayne, *Cinema and Spectatorship* (New York: Routledge Press, 1993); and Linda Williams, ed., *Viewing Position: Ways of Seeing Film* (New Brunswick: Rutgers University Press, 1994).

19. "Pulling Off the Bed Clothes," made by G. W. Bitzer on May 19, 1903. Listed in Niver, *Early Motion Pictures*, with the Library of Congress catalogue entry AM&B, ©H32001, May 19, 1903, FLA 4323. All referenced films from the Paper Print Collection will be listed in this manner.

Chapter Two. The Adjustable Bed

1. See particularly Carroll Smith Rosenberg, "The Female World of Love and Ritual," and "The New Woman as Androgyne" in *Disorderly Conduct: Visions of Gender in 19th-Century America* (New York: Knopf, 1985), 53–76 and 245–296. See also Elaine Tyler May, *Great Expectations: Marriage and Divorce in Post-Victorian America* (Chicago: University of Chicago Press, 1980); and Peiss, *Cheap Amusements*. For an earlier discussion, see Christine Stansell in *City of Women: Sex and Class in New York, 1789–1860* (New York: Knopf, 1986).

2. For discussions about the construction of heterosexuality, see, for example, Jonathan Katz, *The Invention of Heterosexuality* (New York: Dutton, 1995); and Kevin White, *The First Sexual Revolution: The Emergence of Male Heterosexuality in Modern America* (New York: New York University Press, 1993).

3. Griffith's relationship to the emerging moral code in early film is discussed by many film historians. See, for instance, Robert Lang, *American Film Melodrama: Griffith, Vidor, Minelli* (Princeton: Princeton University Press, 1989); Scott Simmon, *The Films of D. W. Griffith* (Cambridge: Cambridge University Press, 1993); and Hansen, *Babel and Babylon*.

4. Edison, ©H1494, March 1, 1901, FLA3753.

5. Edison, © H1496, March 1, 1901, FLA4759.

6. AM&B, ©H34809, August 19, 1903, FLA4101. Although the film was sent to the Library of Congress for paper print copyright on the date indicated, the collection index listing notes the date of production as 1898, though with a question mark (Niver, *Early Motion Pictures*, 228). It is therefore possible that the film predates the Edison version, but there is really no way to know. In either circumstance, it is clear that the humor was popular enough at the turn of the century to warrant multiple versions.

7. See for example "The Old Maid and the Burglar," AM&B, ©H34514, August 13, 1903, FLA3579; "The Old Maid's Disappointment," AM&B, ©H19651, July 2, 1902, FLA3794; and "The Old Maid and the Fortune Teller," Edison, ©H42206, February 16, 1904, FLA4758.

8. "The Disappointed Old Maid," AM&B, ©H32632, June 13, 1903, FLA3584.

9. See Daniel Scott Smith, "Family Limitation, Sexual Control, and Domestic Feminism in Victorian America," in Mary Hartmann and Lois Banner, eds., *Clio's Consciousness Raised: New Perspectives on the History of Women* (New York: Harper and Row, 1974), 121.

10. See Sheila Jeffreys, *The Spinster and Her Enemies* (London: Pandora Press, 1985), for a discussion of this issue in England. See also Nina Auerbach, *Woman and the Demon: The Life of a Victorian Myth* (Cambridge: Cambridge University Press, 1982).

11. See Jane Stedman, "From Dame to Woman: W. S. Gilbert and Theatrical Transvestism," in Martha Vicinus, ed., *Suffer and Be Still: Women in the Victorian Age* (Bloomington: Indiana University Press, 1972), 20–37. There are limits to how far this comparison to the American old maid can go. Much more formally ingrained class structures and tensions, as well as a public concern for "surplus women" in England as early as mid-century, make the British Dame a differently "loaded" satiric icon, even if some surface similarities, such as severity of appearance and male portrayal, invite comparison.

12. Original witchcraft assaults dating back to the Middle Ages specifically claimed female "oversexuality" as primary evidence of magic practices. As the anti-witch tradition moved to England, Scotland, and then America, female witches were imbued with a variety of magical autonomous powers, some overtly sexual, some more subtly so. See Carol Karlsen, *The Devil in the Shape of a Woman: Witchcraft in Colonial New England* (New York: Norton, 1987); John Demos, *Entertaining Satan: Witchcraft and the Culture of Early New England* (New York: Oxford University Press, 1982); Ann Kibbee, "Mutations of the Supernatural: Witchcraft, Remarkable Providences, and the Power of Puritan Men," in *American Quarterly* 34 (Summer 1982): 125–148; and Elizabeth Reiss, "The Devil, the Body, and the Feminine Soul in Puritan New England," *Journal of American History* 82 (June 1995): 15–36.

13. See discussion in chapter 3, note 6.

14. Released first by Edison, © H73465, December 16, 1898, FLA3066. It was remade by Edison on September 11, 1901, at twice the original length (at least twice as much footage exists in the Library of Congress), ©H8587, FLA4946.

15. AM&B, ©H60292, May 3, 1905, FLA4105.

16. See chapter 3.

17. See Patricia A. Vertinsky, *The Eternally Wounded Woman: Women, Doctors, and Exercise in the Late Nineteenth Century* (Urbana: University of Illinois Press, 1994); Martha H. Verbrugge, *Able-bodied Womanhood: Personal Health and Social Change in Nineteenth-Century Boston* (New

York: Oxford University Press, 1988); John S. and Robin M. Haller, *The Physician and Sexuality in Victorian America* (Urbana: University of Illinois Press, 1974).

18. "The Physical Culture Lesson," AM&B, ©H78531, June 1, 1906, FLA3599. Bitzer was particularly interested in the subject. Three years earlier, also for American Mutascope and Biograph, he made three short films on the same day of different women doing various exercises: "The Physical Culture Girl, no. 1," AM&B, ©H33644, July 21, 1903, FLA3458; "The Physical Culture Girl, no. 2," AM&B, ©H33645, July 21, 1903, FLA3459; "The Physical Culture Girl, no. 3," AM&B, ©H33646, July 21, 1903, FLA3460.

19. "The Athletic Girl and the Burglar, no. 1," AM&B, ©H60295, May 3, 1905, FLA4481; "The Athletic Girl and the Burglar, no. 2," AM&B, ©H60296, May 3, 1905, FLA4049.

20. Edwin S. Porter made another version for Edison a few months later, "The Physical Culture Girl," Edison, ©H36499, October 3, 1903, FLA5168.

21. See, for example, "The Pajama Girl," AM&B, ©H32109, May 22, 1903 (photographed by G. W. Bitzer), FLA3737; "The Pajama Statue Girls," AM&B, ©H38861, December 5, 1903 (photographed by A. E. Weed), FLA4186; "The Soubrette's Slide," AM&B, ©H42175, February 15, 1904 (photographed by A. E. Weed), FLA4043; or one that might appear on a television talk show today, "They Meet on the Mat," AM&B, ©H79738, June 19, 1906 (photographed by, of course, G. W. Bitzer), FLA3839.

22. "Love in a Hammock," Edison, ©H375, January 12, 1901, FLA3697; "Three Girls in a Hammock," AM&B, ©H41043, January 20, 1904 (photographed by A. E. Weed), FLA4335; "The Adjustable Bed," AM&B, ©H61112, May 19, 1905 (photographed by G. W. Bitzer), FLA3786; "Always Room for One More," AM&B, ©H65316, September 11, 1905 (photographed by G. W. Bitzer), FLA3909.

23. The historian utilizes statutory rape testimony with care, keeping in mind several important caveats. The courtrooms and bedrooms of towns such as Sacramento reflected and reinforced the power relations that governed men and women. When reading statutory rape trial testimony, one cannot escape the reality that no equality of position existed between the "victim" and the defendant, despite the consensual nature of the crime. The recognition that men in their twenties held more power, both in the society and in their personal relationships, than did women in their teens is part of what led to the statutory rape laws. Uncovering more complicated meanings in the testimony does not obviate the truth of that power inequity. It is equally important to note that the judicial system, in bringing its immense authority to bear when prosecuting these sex crimes, altered the nature of the discourse that emerged, and the testimony needs to be read carefully.

24. Case #1615, Amendment to Bill of Exceptions, 6–7. Records of Superior Court, Criminal Division, County of Sacramento, Sacramento City Archives.

25. Ibid., 24.

26. Ibid., 28.

27. Ibid., 27.

28. Ibid., 24.

29. Ibid., 4.

30. Case #1615, Judge's Instructions. Records of Superior Court, Criminal Division, County of Sacramento, Sacramento City Archives.

31. Ibid.

32. Case #4793, Records of Superior Court, Criminal Division, County of Sacramento, Sacramento City Archives. Primary testimony to be found in Grand Jury Transcript in the matter of John Salle, Monday, November 14, 1910. Unless otherwise indicated, all page numbers refer to the Grand Jury transcript.

33. Ibid., 23, judge's remarks upon sentencing.

34. Ibid., 19.

35. Ibid.

36. Ibid., 23.

37. Ibid., 28. The Eagle restaurant figures prominently in a variety of sex-crime cases. It clearly functioned as a quasi-illicit place at which young people could gather away from parental eyes.

38. Ibid., 1, 35–37.

39. Ibid., 7.

40. Ibid., 32–33.

41. Ibid., 33.

42. Ibid., 41.

43. Mabel Springer and Pete Kostena were acquitted. There is no record of the charge, but one assumes it was contributing to the delinquency of a minor. Salle, as noted, was sentenced to five years. There is no record of what happened to Almary Jones.

44. Case #4793, 24, judge's remarks upon sentencing.

45. See Peiss, *Cheap Amusements*, for an excellent discussion of this phenomenon in the major urban areas.

46. Case #5006, Statement under §1192a, California Penal Code, 4. Records of Superior Court, Criminal Division, County of Sacramento, Sacramento City Archives.

47. Ibid., 3.

48. Ibid., 2.

49. Case #5006, Transcript of Grand Jury Testimony taken February 6, 1912, 9. Records of Superior Court, Criminal Division, County of Sacramento, Sacramento City Archives.

50. Ibid.

51. Case #5006, Statement under §1192a, California Penal Code, 3.

52. Case #5006, Grand Jury Transcript, 16.

53. Ibid.

54. Ibid., 21.

55. Case #5006, Statement under §1192a, California Penal Code, Probation Officer's Report, 13.

56. Case #5006, Statement under §1192a, California Penal Code, Judge's Sentencing Remarks, 16.

57. Ibid., 17.

58. Cases #5415, 5416. Records of Superior Court, Criminal Division, County of Sacramento, Sacramento City Archives.

59. For further examples of this phenomenon in Sacramento, look to Case #1812 and #4473 (from 1898 and 1908, respectively), wherein the jury refused to convict under similar circumstances. See Case #4699 in 1910, #5252 in 1913, and #5261, a group prosecution of eight men the same year, for examples of the by-now standard probation. Records of Superior Court, Criminal Division, County of Sacramento, Sacramento City Archives.

Chapter Three.
The Twentieth-Century Way

1. *Variety*, 24 April 1909, 12.

2. *New York Evening World*, 10 March 1914, Robinson Locke Scrapbooks, Ser. 3, v. 431, 129. Billy Rose Theatre Collection, New York Public Library.

3. Letter from Eugene Fisher to C. V. McClatchy, 20 November 1914, 2. Also *Sacramento Bee* Long Beach Investigation (see note 75 below).

4. See, for example, E. Anthony Rotundo, *American Manhood: Transformations in Masculinity from the Revolution to the Modern Era* (New York: Basic Books, 1993); J. A. Mangin and James Walvin, eds., *Manliness and Morality: Middle Class Manhood in Britain and America, 1800 to 1940* (New York: St. Martin's Press, 1987); Mark C. Carnes and Clyde Griffen, eds., *Meanings for Manhood: Constructions of Masculinity in Victorian America* (Chicago: University of Chicago Press, 1990); and White, *The First Sexual Revolution*.

5. See particularly Richard von Krafft-Ebing, *Psychopathia Sexualis*, trans. Charles Gilbert Chaddock (Philadelphia: F. A. Davis, 1893); and Havelock Ellis, *Studies in the Psychology of Sex* (New York: Random House, [1906], 1936). A spirited historical response to the power of the sexologists can be found in George Chauncey, "From Sexual Inversion to Homosexuality: Medicine and the Changing Conceptualization of Female Deviance," *Salamagundi* 58–59 (Fall/Winter 1982–1983): 114–146. Chauncey also addresses the problem of these complicated discourses in "Christian Brotherhood or Sexual Perversion? Homosexual Identities and the Construction of Sexual Boundaries in the World War One Era," *Journal of Social History* 19 (1985): 189–211, and in *Gay New York*. See also Jeffrey Weeks, *Sexuality and Its Discontents: Meanings, Myths and Modern Sexualities* (London: Routledge and Kegan Paul, 1985). See Carroll Smith Rosenberg, "The New Woman as Androgyne," in *Disorderly Conduct*; Lillian Faderman, "The Morbidification of Love Between Women by 19th-Century Sexologists," *Journal of Homosexuality* 4 (1978): 73–90; and Esther Newton, "The Myth of the Mannish Lesbian," in Freedman et al., eds., *The Lesbian Issue: Essays from Signs* (Chicago: University of Chicago Press, 1985), 7–25, for discussions of the sexologists' impact on women.

6. Both female and *male* impersonation hit a peak in this era. Although this discussion is limited to female impersonation, my research uncovered an extended network of male impersonators. Although female impersonation seemed more popular and generated more performers, significant female stars who impersonated men included Vesta Tilly, Kitty Donner, Kathleen Clifford, Ella Shields, Bessie Bonehill, and Hetty King, to name a few. The discussion about their activity sometimes matched that about their male counterparts, but significant differences existed. Though questions of sexual deviancy did arise, other issues not present in female impersonation appeared as well—particularly concerns over public politics and the relationship between, for example, male impersonation and the highly contentious suffrage movement. Additionally, whereas female impersonators were judged by how well they presented the image of adult women, male impersonators were assessed by their embodiment of "the boy." This diminution reinforces the fact that much of the discourse surrounding gender impersonation in what was essentially a male-produced press focused primarily upon notions of masculinity in one form or another. Commentators questioned whether female impersonators were really men and gave male impersonators only the status of boys.

7. See Toll, *On with the Show*, chapter 9. See also Marybeth Hamilton, "'I'm the Queen of the Bitches': Female Impersonation and Mae West's

Pleasure Man," found in Lesley Ferris, ed., *Crossing the Stage: Controversies on Cross Dressing* (London and New York: Routledge, 1993).

8. Toll, *On with the Show*, 240.

9. For a fine discussion of the relationship between class, gender, and minstrelsy, see Eric Lott, *Love and Theft: Blackface Minstrelsy and the American Working Class* (New York: Oxford University Press, 1993). For an earlier treatment, see Robert C. Toll, *Blacking Up: The Minstrel Show in Nineteenth Century America* (New York: Oxford University Press, 1974).

10. Slide, *The Vaudevillians*, 51.

11. For an extended discussion of performativity in gender, see Judith Butler's groundbreaking *Gender Trouble: Feminism and the Subversion of Identity* (New York: Routledge, 1990). See also Judith Butler, *Bodies That Matter: On the Discursive Limits of Sex* (New York: Routledge, 1993).

12. *Variety*, 24 April 1909, 12.

13. *Variety*, 23 April 1910, 12.

14. Ibid.

15. *Variety*, 4 February 1911, 4.

16. *Variety*, 1 June 1912, 11; *Variety*, 8 November 1912, 10.

17. See Slide, *The Vaudevillians*, 17–18, for a general discussion of Browne's career. See also Toll, *On with the Show*, chapter 9.

18. See Toll, *On with the Show*, chapter 9. For a discussion of vaudeville theatre circuits, see Snyder, *The Voice of the City*, and Dimeglio, *Vaudeville U.S.A.*

19. *Variety*, 20 September 1912, 2.

20. Ibid., 26.

21. *Variety*, 11 October 1912, 20.

22. *Variety*, 18 October 1912, 28.

23. *Variety*, 4 October 1912, 17, 18.

24. *Variety*, 23 August 1912, 20.

25. *Variety*, 16 August 1912, 21.

26. *New York Review*, 1 October 1910, in Bothwell Browne Clippings File, Billy Rose Collection, New York Public Library.

27. *Variety*, 23 April 1910, 12.

28. Ibid.

29. Unmarked clipping, 11 April 1913, Robinson Locke Scrapbooks, Ser. 3, v. 431, 78.

30. Ibid., 24–25.

31. *Cincinnati Times Star*, 7 March 1912, Robinson Locke Scrapbooks, Ser. 3, v. 431, 19.

32. Ibid. Readers should no doubt hold some skepticism about the veracity of these quotes. Entertainment reporters commonly made up such

stories. Nevertheless, even if the quote is fictional, the reporter obviously thought he was identifying Eltinge's appeal, and other comments from contemporary reviewers and critics support this particular journalist's understanding.

33. *Cincinnati Times Star*, 11 January 1915, Robinson Locke Scrapbooks, Ser. 3, v. 431, 181.

34. *St. Louis Globe*, 11 March 1912, Robinson Locke Scrapbooks, Ser. 3, v. 431, 18.

35. There are three issues of the *Julian Eltinge Magazine* in the Townshend Walsh Collection at the New York Public Library. They are undated but appear to be from 1912–1913. Two are entitled the *Julian Eltinge Magazine*. One of these has a "#3" on the cover; the other has "2" penciled on it. A third issue is entitled the *Julian Eltinge Magazine and Beauty Hints*.

36. Unmarked typescript press release dated 1912, Julian Eltinge Clippings File, Billy Rose Theatre Collection, New York Public Library.

37. *Cincinnati Times Star*, 7 March 1912, Julian Eltinge Clipping File.

38. *Variety*, 24 April 1909, 12.

39. *Milwaukee Journal*, undated, Julian Eltinge Clipping File.

40. *Julian Eltinge Magazine*, Number 3, Townshend Walsh Collection.

41. *Variety*, 24 April 1909, 12.

42. *Cincinnati Times Star*, Julian Eltinge Clipping File.

43. Unmarked clipping, Julian Eltinge Clipping File.

44. *Boston Traveler*, 18 May 1912, Robinson Locke Scrapbooks, Ser. 2, v. 160, 91.

45. Ibid.

46. *Cincinnati Commercial*, 28 February 1912, Robinson Locke Scrapbooks, Ser. 3, v. 431, 10.

47. *Toledo Blade*, 24 February 1912, Robinson Locke Scrapbooks, Ser. 3, v. 431, 37.

48. Unmarked press release dated 1912 found in Julian Eltinge Clipping File.

49. Unmarked clipping, 6 June 1913, Robinson Locke Scrapbooks, Ser. 2, v. 160, 108.

50. Anthony Slide, *The Great Pretenders: A History of Female and Male Impersonation in the Performing Arts* (Lombard: Wallace-Homestead Book Co., 1986), 21 and 24.

51. *Variety*, 16 September 1911, 20.

52. *Dramatic Mirror*, 16 August 1921, 663.

53. *Boston Transcript*, 30 April 1912, Robinson Locke Scrapbooks, Ser. 3, v. 431, 40.

54. Unmarked clipping dated 21 March 1914, Robinson Locke Scrapbooks, Ser. 3, v. 431, 127.

55. Ibid.

56. *Boston Traveler*, 18 May 1912, Robinson Locke Scrapbooks, Ser. 2, v. 160, 91.

57. Ibid.

58. *Stage Pictorial*, June 1913, Robinson Locke Scrapbooks, Ser. 3, v. 431, 85.

59. *New York Evening World*, 10 March 1914, Robinson Locke Scrapbooks, Ser. 3, v. 431, 129.

60. Unmarked source, probably *Dramatic Mirror* or *NY Telegraph*, Bothwell Browne Clipping File, Billy Rose Collection, New York Public Library.

61. Unmarked source, 4 October 1910, Bothwell Browne Clipping File.

62. *Los Angeles Examiner*, 24 May 1913, Bothwell Browne Clipping File.

63. Ibid.

64. *The Detroit News*, 10 September 1913, Robinson Locke Scrapbooks, Ser. 3, v. 431, 88.

65. Ibid.

66. Ibid.

67. As historian Robert Toll noted in his 1976 survey of American popular entertainment, numerous contemporary commentators subjected Eltinge and his ilk to similarly bitter criticism that specifically called forth images of "degeneracy" in Europe and the Middle East. Toll concluded that "whether impersonators were homosexuals . . . and . . . disqualified from being performers were the underlying questions in the controversy surrounding them." See Toll, *On with the Show*, 249.

68. Case #1833, Records of Superior Court, Criminal Division, County of Sacramento, Sacramento City Archives.

69. Case #4155, #4154, and #4153, Jury Instructions, Records of Superior Court, Criminal Division, County of Sacramento, Sacramento City Archives. See also *Sacramento Bee*, 16 July 1906, for specific reference to John Kagee's trial.

70. *Sacramento Bee*, 22 July 1906.

71. *Sacramento Bee*, 12 July 1906.

72. Case #4332; also *Sacramento Bee*, 20 July 1907.

73. Case #4338; also *Sacramento Bee*, 18 July 1907.

74. Social vagrancy was a catch-all charge used to arrest a large variety of community offenders. People who had no visible means of support, traveling salesmen, "loose" women, and generally unpleasant characters found themselves subject to arrest as social vagrants.

75. *Sacramento Bee*, 23 November 1914, as reprinted in an unmarked clipping. Found in uncatalogued investigations file held by the Sacramento City Archives (hereafter referred to as the *Sacramento Bee* Long Beach Investigation). This uncatalogued file was brought to my attention by James Henley, director of the Sacramento City Archives. It contains numerous letters between McClatchy and Fisher, drafts of proposed articles by Fisher, Fisher's original notes on his conversations with Long Beach police detectives and his prime source, L. L. Rollins, and a photograph of an unidentified gentleman dressed in a lovely frock. As of April 1996, the file remained uncatalogued.

76. Although McClatchy's obsession with the case is never explained, it may have something to do with the fact that a former Sacramento minister was netted in the Long Beach raid. A Reverend Baker, forced out of his Sacramento church for unstated reasons in 1907, somehow found his way to Long Beach. McClatchy asked Fisher to find out any specific details that he could concerning Baker's circumstances.

77. Testimony of Herbert N. Lowe at his trial for social vagrancy as reported in a transmittal from Fisher to the *Sacramento Bee*, 11 December 1914, *Sacramento Bee* Long Beach Investigation.

78. Rollins claimed 5,000; the police assumed he was exaggerating and speculated 2,000. Letter from Fisher to McClatchy, 5 December 1914, *Sacramento Bee* Long Beach Investigation.

79. Transmittal from Eugene Fisher to *Sacramento Bee*, undated but appears to be late November 1914. The quoted passage appears on page 13 of the transmittal, which opens with the following quotation from *Hamlet* (Act III, Scene 4): "Such an act that blurs the blush and grace of Modesty, takes off the rose from the fair forehead of innocent youth and sets a blister there." Hereinafter referred to as Shakespeare Transmittal.

80. Shakespeare Transmittal, 10.

81. Ibid., 11.

82. Ibid.

83. Ibid., 12.

84. Transmittal from Fisher to McClatchy dated 20 November 1914, 4.

85. Shakespeare Transmittal, 3–4.

86. Ibid., 14.

87. Convictions for crimes against nature (a statute on the California books since 1850) were repeatedly challenged on the grounds that the statute was too vague and did not specify whether its provisions covered oral sex. The California legislature responded in 1915 by enacting section 288a of the penal code, which specifically declared fellatio and cunnilingus to be felonies punishable by up to fifteen years in prison. See Allan Berubè,

"Sodomy and Sex Perversion Laws in California Since 1850" (paper presented to the Bay Area Lawyers for Individual Freedom, January 30, 1986). Berubè points out that the law was overturned by the California Supreme Court a few years later because it violated a new anti-Spanish amendment to the state constitution that required all laws to be written in English. Apparently cunnilingus and fellatio could not be found in an English-language dictionary. The California legislature rectified their linguistic oversight in 1921 and made oral sex a felony in English as well as Latin.

88. Letter from Fisher to McClatchy, 20 November 1914, 1.

89. Shakespeare Transmittal, 5.

90. Ibid.

91. Ibid., 6.

92. Letter from Fisher to McClatchy, 20 November 1914, 2.

93. Shakespeare Transmittal, 12.

94. Ibid.

95. Ibid., 6, 10, and 12.

96. See George Chauncey, *Gay New York*, and Freedman and D'Emilio, *Intimate Matters*, for an overview. See also Eric Garber, "A Spectacle in Color: The Lesbian and Gay Subculture of Jazz Age Harlem," in Duberman, Vicinus, & Chauncey Jr., eds., *Hidden from History: Reclaiming the Gay and Lesbian Past* (New York: New American Library, 1989), 318–331.

97. Shakespeare Transmittal, 2, 18. Also letter from Fisher to McClatchy, 5 December 1914. Fisher claimed that Brown and Warren were negotiating with San Diego authorities and planned to continue their work in San Francisco, Sacramento, Portland, Seattle, Chicago, Boston, and New York. I have found no further trace of them, however.

98. Fisher to McClatchy, 20 November 1914, 2–3. For an extended discussion of early-twentieth-century police surveillance tactics in cases of homosexual prosecution, see Steven J. Maynard, "Through a Hole in the Lavatory Wall: Homosexual Subcultures, Police Sureveillance, and the Dialectics of Discovery, Toronto, 1890–1930," *Journal of the History of Sexuality* 5 (1994): 207–242.

99. Shakespeare Transmittal, 20. This paragraph was specifically slashed by an editor.

100. Fisher to McClatchy, 5 December 1914, 1.

101. Unmarked news clipping, *Sacramento Bee* Long Beach Investigation.

102. Shakespeare Transmittal, 11.

103. Fisher to McClatchy, 20 November 1914, 2.

104. Unmarked clipping, *Sacramento Bee* Long Beach Investigation.

105. Loose photograph, *Sacramento Bee* Long Beach Investigation.

106. Shakespeare Transmittal, 22. The context clearly denotes the word "powdered."

107. Loose transmittal sheet from Fisher to *Sacramento Bee* labeled "p. 2." It begins with the phrase "Startling disclosures have been made" and appears to be either an earlier draft or a rewrite of a portion of the Shakespeare Transmittal.

Chapter Four. Why Mr. Nation
Wants a Divorce

1. Edison, ©H1495, March 1, 1901, FLA4951.

2. See Janet Farrell Brodie, *Contraception and Abortion in Nineteenth-Century America* (Ithaca: Cornell University Press, 1994); Carole R. McCann, *Birth Control Politics in the United States, 1916–1945* (Ithaca: Cornell University Press, 1994); J. A. and Olive Banks, *Feminism and Family Planning in Victorian England* (New York: Schocken Books, 1964); Daniel Scott Smith, "Family Limitation, Sexual Control, and Domestic Feminism," in Hartmann and Banner, eds., *Clio's Consciousness Raised*, 119–136; and D'Emilio and Freedman, *Intimate Matters*, 58–59.

3. *Variety*, 6 August 1910, 12.

4. AM&B, ©H70259, December 19, 1905, FLA5235. Although copyrighted as "The Threshing Scene," the film was released in 1906 under the title "The Henpecked Husband."

5. AM&B, ©H89469, January 17, 1907, FLA5758.

6. AM&B, ©H36630, October 8, 1903, FLA3115.

7. AM&B, ©H27830, January 22, 1903 (August 18, 1899 filming date), FLA3284.

8. AM&B, ©H104043, December 24, 1907, FLA5577.

9. AM&B, ©J146452, October 14, 1910, FLA5562.

10. "The Unfaithful Wife: Part 1, The Lover," AM&B, ©H33877, July 28, 1903, FLA4096.

11. "The Unfaithful Wife: Part 2, The Fight," AM&B, ©H33878, July 28, 1903, FLA4097.

12. "The Unfaithful Wife: Part 3, Murder and Suicide," AM&B, ©H33879, July 28, 1903, FLA4098.

13. "The Message," Biograph, ©J129505, July 6, 1909, FLA5569; "The Better Way," Biograph, ©J130564, August 13, 1909, FLA4905.

14. *Variety*, 21 July 1906, 12; *Variety*, 4 August 1906, 8.

15. *Boston Herald*, 19 May 1912, Locke Envelope 1725, Robinson Locke Scrapbooks, Billy Rose Collection, New York Public Library.

16. Unidentified news clipping dated 2 November 1906, Harry Bulgur Clippings File, Billy Rose Collection, New York Public Library.

17. "And A Little Child Shall Lead Them," AM&B, ©H123958, March 13, 1909, FLA4415; "A Child's Stratagem," Biograph, ©J148630, December 9, 1910, FLA 5294.

18. "The Divorce: Detected," AM&B, ©H33410, June 13, 1903, FLA4084; "The Divorce: On the Trail," AM&B, ©H33411, June 13, 1903, FLA4086; "The Divorce: Evidence Secured," AM&B, ©H3341, June 13, 1903, FLA4085.

19. Edison, ©H1495, March 1, 1901, FLA4951.

20. Although female initiation of divorce has sometimes been portrayed in history as evidence of male chivalry, deposition testimony in Sacramento does not support this idea. Countless genuine desertions, where the defendant cannot be found despite repeated attempts, fill the files, and the testimony that does appear is often so rancorous on both sides that one is hardpressed to uncover civility, let alone chivalry.

21. See particularly Glenda Riley, *Divorce: An American Tradition* (New York: Oxford University Press, 1991); May, *Great Expectations*; Robert L. Griswold, *Family and Divorce in California, 1850–1890: Victorian Illusions and Everyday Realities* (Albany: State University of New York Press, 1982); and William O'Neill, *Divorce in the Progressive Era* (New Haven: Yale University Press, 1967).

22. Roderick Phillips, *Putting Asunder: A History of Divorce in Western Society* (Cambridge: Cambridge University Press, 1988), 462.

23. Ibid., 463, xi; see also chapter 14:1,2 for an extended discussion of the complexity behind the production of statistics on divorce. By all counts, though, in the late twentieth century anywhere from 30 to 50 percent of all marriages ended in legal dissolution.

24. Felix Adler, *Marriage and Divorce* (New York: D. Appleton and Company, [1905] reprint 1915), 13.

25. Ibid., 21.

26. See Paula Fass, *The Damned and the Beautiful: American Youth in the 1920s* (Oxford: Oxford University Press, 1977); Ellen Kay Trimberger, ed., *Intimate Warriors: Portraits of a Modern Marriage, 1899–1944* (New York: Feminist Press at the City University of New York, 1991); and Barbara Epstein, "Family, Sexual Morality, and Popular Movements in Turn of the Century America," in Ann Snitow, Christine Stansell, and Sharon Thompson, eds., *Powers of Desire: The Politics of Sexuality* (New York: Monthly Review Press, 1983), 117–130.

27. See Karen Lystra, *Searching the Heart: Women, Men, and Romantic Love in Nineteenth-Century America* (New York: Oxford University Press,

1989); Peter Gay, *The Bourgeois Experience, Victoria to Freud*, Vol. 1, *Education of the Senses* (New York: Oxford University Press, 1984).

28. See Mary Somerville Jones, "An Historical Geography of Changing Divorce Law in the United States" (Ph.D. dissertation, University of North Carolina, 1978). See also the first authoritative analysis, Alfred Cahen, *Statistical Analysis of American Divorce* (New York: Columbia University Press, 1932).

29. Somerville Jones, "Historical Geography," 46–66.

30. Data drawn from 275 cases. All divorces for the sample years 1895 and 1905 were studied, as were two miscellaneous sets of documents with missing forms separately filed for the years 1895–1898 and 1905–1908. In 1895, 84 percent of cases identified the location of the marriage. Of these, 66 percent had married in California—fully 46 percent in Sacramento itself. Statistics for 1905 are similar. Eighty-one percent of cases identified marriage location; of these, 74 percent married in California, 47 percent in Sacramento. By 1905, 33 percent of the out-of-state divorces were granted to individuals who had immigrated from overseas. It seems unlikely that they sought out California purely for a liberal divorce policy.

31. Records of Sacramento Superior Court, Civil Division, County of Sacramento, 1895–1896, 1905–1906.

32. See Somerville Jones, "Historical Geography," 58.

33. The average length of marriage for those obtaining a divorce in Sacramento was 8.2 years. That figure remained absolutely static between 1895 and 1905 despite a 12 percent increase in the number of divorces.

34. Case #6504, Sacramento Superior Court, Civil Division, County of Sacramento, Sacramento City Archives.

35. Ibid., Judge's Ruling, 3.

36. Ibid., 6.

37. Ibid., 4.

38. Ibid., 5.

39. Ibid.

40. Ibid., 6. The case cited by the judge is identified only as *Conant vs. Conant*, 10 Cal. 249 (found on p. 5 of ruling).

41. Ibid., 1.

42. Ibid., 6.

43. Case #6504, Defendant's Cross-Complaint, 8.

44. Case #6504, Judge's Ruling, 6.

45. Case #6504, Defendant's Cross-Complaint, 8.

46. Case #6504, Judge's Ruling, 6.

47. Ibid., 6–7.

48. Ibid., 8.

49. Ibid., 9.

50. Case #6504, Defendant's Cross-Complaint, 16.

51. Ibid., 7.

52. Ibid., 4. The APA organization is not otherwise identified, and I have been unable to find it listed formally in Sacramento. The context of the accusation clearly references her refusal to have children, and this may have been a small group of Sacramento women working quietly for birth control.

53. Case #6504, Defendant's Cross-Complaint, 8–9.

54. Ibid., 9.

55. See John S. and Robin M. Haller, *The Physician and Sexuality in Victorian America* (Urbana: University of Illinois Press, 1974). On page 101 of the paperback edition (New York: Norton, 1977), the Hallers make this point, and in footnote #27 they cite as their sources Alexander Walker, *Intermarriage: Or the Mode in Which and the Causes Why Beauty, Health, and Intellect Result from Certain Unions, and Deformity, Disease and Insanity From Others* (New York: n.p., 1839), 256; and William M. Capp, *The Daughter: Her Health, Education and Wedlock* (Philadelphia: n.p., 1891), 94.

56. See Robert L. Griswold, "The Evolution of the Doctrine of Mental Cruelty in Victorian American Divorce, 1790–1900," *Journal of Social History* 20 (Fall 1986): 127–148, for a discussion of the legal history behind the cruelty doctrine.

57. This rhetoric is troublesome. Violent-assault rape received little prosecutorial attention. In Progressive-Era courts, prosecution for rape almost always emerged from statutory age violations (unless racial miscegenation was alleged). Assault rape, when prosecuted, often appeared under the charge of general assault, thus removing the sexual nature of the crime. Although this may have been done to protect the female victim, ultimately it fostered the belief that women could not be raped.

58. Case #6844, *John T. Stoll v. Ursula*, Complaint, 2. Sacramento Superior Court, Civil Division, County of Sacramento, Sacramento City Archives.

59. Case #10956, *Roy A. Morten v. Anita*, Complaint, 2.

60. Case #11079, *Charles G. Landes v. Sylvia V.*, Complaint, 1.

61. Case #11027, *W. N. Morris v. S. S.*, Complaint, 2.

62. Case #6504, *Ella Riley v. John*, Ruling, 7. Ella Riley denied these charges, and the judge did not mention them as fact in his ruling.

63. See in particular May, *Great Expectations*.

64. This was one of the more interesting appellations that arose. Most name-calling references were both repetitive and quite familiar to a late-twentieth-century ear. "SOB, bastard, bitch" all appeared so often that my

first impulse was to assume that a formula existed in divorce law by which to demonstrate cruel conduct. Yet every now and then an odd phrase, usually an ethnic slur, popped up, and I felt reassured of the veracity. "Whoremaster" came up frequently, although not uniformly, and I had never heard it before outside of nineteenth-century novels. In the beginning I assumed it to be a stock inclusion on advice of counsel, but its pattern of erratic entry into the documents convinced me that it must have been a fairly common turn-of-the-century insult that, unlike the others, fell into disuse.

65. This is a problematic accusation. Forcing one's wife into prostitution was a felony and constituted a specific ground for divorce under California law. Although the allegation usually appears within the complaint and is not formally offered as one of the grounds, it may have been thrown in as a backup strategy. However, this is not an accusation that appears with any frequency, thus casting some doubt on the idea that it merely served as a tactic.

66. Case #11152, *Hattie M. Mohwinkel v. John H.*, Complaint, 6. Sacramento Superior Court, Civil Division, County of Sacramento, Sacramento City Archives.

67. Case #8014, *Mary Harrison v. Thomas*, Complaint, 3–5.

68. Case #10832, *Ida D. Harwood v. William H.*, Complaint, 3–4.

69. Case #12064, *Emma Malcolm v. Clarence*, Complaint, 4. The omission of the word "fuck," clearly the absent reference, was unusual for a divorce deposition. Virtually everything was said outright in these documents.

70. Case #11255, *Lucy R. Wing v. Frank*, Complaint, 3.

71. Case #11680, *Mary Elizabeth Grant v. William E.*, Complaint, 3.

72. See Rosen, *Lost Sisterhood: Prostitution in America 1900–1918* (Baltimore: Johns Hopkins University Press, 1982), for what is still one of the best treatments of this subject; also Barbara Meil Hobson, *Uneasy Virtue: The Politics of Prostitution and the American Reform Tradition* (New York: Basic Books, 1987). See chapter 5 in this book as well.

Chapter Five. The Soubrette's Slide

1. See Timothy J. Gilfoyle, *City of Eros: New York City, Prostitution, and the Commercialization of Sex, 1790–1920* (New York: Norton, 1992); Thomas C. Mackey, *Red Lights Out: A Legal History of Prostitution, Disorderly Houses, and Vice Districts, 1870–1917* (New York: Garland, 1987); David J. Langum, *Crossing Over the Line: Legislating Morality and the Mann Act* (Chicago: The University of Chicago Press, 1994); Rosen, *The*

Lost Sisterhood; Hobson, *Uneasy Virtue*; Marion S. Goldman, *Gold Diggers and Silver Miners: Prostitution and Social Life in the Comstock Lode* (Ann Arbor: University of Michigan Press, 1981); Mark T. Connelly, *The Response to Prostitution in America* (Chapel Hill: University of North Carolina Press, 1980); David Pivar, *Purity Crusade: Sexual Morality and Social Control, 1868–1900* (Westport: Greenwood Press, 1973); and Ann M. Butler, *Daughters of Joy, Sisters of Misery: Prostitutes in the American West, 1865–1890* (Urbana: University of Illinois Press, 1985), to name but a few of the books. Hundreds of articles have been published as well.

2. Krafft-Ebing, Havelock Ellis, and Freud had, of course, all published by this time. Nevertheless, their work was not widely disseminated, even among most of the Progressives, and their work meant nothing to the vast majority of middle- and working-class individuals who found themselves steeped in the controversies over prostitution.

3. See chapter 2.

4. See Judith R. Walkowitz, *Prostitution and Victorian Society: Women, Class and the State* (New York: Cambridge University Press, 1980); Rosen, *The Lost Sisterhood*; and Hobson, *Uneasy Virtue*.

5. See Peiss, *Cheap Amusements*, and Stansell, *City of Women*.

6. See Bernard Sobel, *Burleycue* (New York: Farrar & Rinehart, 1931); Joe Laurie, Jr., *Vaudeville: From the Honky Tonks to the Palace* (New York: Holt, 1953); and DiMeglio, *Vaudeville, U.S.A.* These books repeatedly claim that vaudeville owners, particularly Tony Pastor in the 1870s, successfully cleaned up vaudeville so as to broaden its base to women and families. This is in line with what the theater owners themselves claimed. Though women and children did come and some vaudeville may have been subject to intermittent cleanups, not a year went by without another major editorial or policy initiative aimed at wiping out off-color or suggestive performances in vaudeville. In twenty years' worth of documents, the issue never went away, strongly suggesting that such performances never did either.

7. See Rosen, *Lost Sisterhood*, 47–48, for a discussion of contradictory stereotypes of prostitutes.

8. AM&B, ©H35629, September 12, 1903, FLA3563.

9. AM&B, ©H41027, January 19, 1904, FLA4923.

10. *Webster's New Collegiate Dictionary* (Springfield: G.&C. Merriam Co., 1979), 1102.

11. "A Soubrette's Troubles on a Fifth Avenue Stage," Edison, ©H7986, August 21, 1901, FLA3404; "The Soubrette's Slide," AM&B, ©H42175, February 15, 1904, FLA4043; "The Sleepy Soubrette," AM&B, ©H57147, February 18, 1905, FLA3771.

12. AM&B, ©H29474, March 18, 1903, FLA3630. Niver, in *Early Motion Pictures*, indicates on page 306 that this film was actually made in October 1900. The copyright dates can be misleading, particularly for films done circa 1900; there was haphazard submission to the Library of Congress in the very early years. The subsequent submission of earlier films (particularly those with sexual content) suggests that the films were sufficiently popular that AM&B became concerned over ownership and financial rights. (AM&B was more prone than Edison both to produce risqué films and to submit late copyright requests. It was Thomas Edison, not surprisingly, who initiated the idea of sending paper prints of his movies to the Library of Congress for patent protection.)

13. "The Unfaithful Wife," AM&B, ©H33877, ©H33878, ©H33879, July 28, 1903, FLA4096, FLA4097, FLA4098; "The Unfaithful Wife" had three "chapters," each registered separately. "The Downward Path" had five: AM&B, ©H23807, ©H23810, ©H23808, ©H23806, ©H23809, November 11, 1902, FLA4011, FLA4014, FLA4012, FLA4010, FLA4013. The numbering reflects the sequential "chapters," despite the nonsequential copyright and shelf location information.

14. AM&B, ©H23808, November 11, 1902, FLA4012; AM&B, ©H23806, November 11, 1902, FLA4010.

15. "The Gerry Society's Mistake," AM&B, ©H39907, December 23, 1903, FLA4262; "The Chorus Girls and the Salvation Army Lassie," AM&B, ©H35630, September 12, 1903, FLA4545.

16. Musser, *The Emergence of Cinema*, 200, 228.

17. Niver, *Early Motion Pictures*, 15. This is under the description of "At the Dressmaker's," AM&B, ©H36557, October 6, 1903, FLA3099.

18. "Mr. Jack in the Dressing Room," AM&B, ©H44028, March 29, 1904, FLA3113; "Peeping Tom in the Dressing Room," AM&B, ©H60655, May 9, 1905, FLA3917; "A Scrap in the Dressing Room," AM&B, ©H40812, January 12, 1904, FLA3936; and "A Scene Behind the Scenes," AM&B, ©H40811, January 12, 1904, FLA3662, all from 1904 and 1905, provide a representative sample. The others discussed in the context of the use of burlesque and soubrette images also qualify in this category.

19. "At the Dressmaker's," AM&B, ©H36557, October 6, 1903, FLA3099; "The Dressmaker's Accident," AM&B, ©H39141, December 7, 1903, FLA4294. The Niver catalogue cross-references the latter film with "Her New Party Gown," AM&B, ©H39140, FLA4337, filmed and released by the same artist (A. E. Weed) on the same day. Niver describes this film as depicting three women in a dressmaker's cutting room who begin to undress a fourth woman in preparation for her fitting (Niver, *Early Motion Pictures*, 135). This film quite obviously falls into the same category as

those under discussion here. (G. W. Bitzer was the cameraman on "At the Dressmaker's.")

20. "The Way to Sell Corsets," AM&B, ©H42036, February 11, 1904, FLA3959; "A Busy Day for the Corset Models," AM&B, ©H42037, February 11, 1904, FLA3407.

21. AM&B, ©H40807, January 12, 1904, FLA3764.

22. "On the Beach at Brighton," AM&B, ©H63380, July 15, 1905, FLA3934; "The Boarding House Bathroom," AM&B, ©H60287, May 3, 1905, FLA3790.

23. Although this discussion has focused extensively on film, it should be recognized that the traveling vaudeville stage also contained this imagery. Many of these early movies came directly from filmed vaudeville acts.

24. In fact, some women were charged with keeping a house of prostitution, although these cases were usually dropped.

25. Case #5261, Transcript of Preliminary Hearing, August 29, 1913, 3. Records of Superior Court, Criminal Division, County of Sacramento, Sacramento City Archives.

26. Ibid., 25–30.

27. Ibid., 24–25.

28. Case #5621, Transcript, 31.

29. Ibid., 37.

30. Ibid., 39.

31. Ibid., 44.

32. Ibid., 46.

33. Ibid., 49–50.

34. Ibid., 52.

35. Ibid., 55–56.

36. Ibid., 63.

37. Ibid., Terms of Probation.

38. Case #5196, Transcript of Preliminary Hearing. Testimony taken February 17, 1913; March 10, 1913; March 11, 1913; March 13, 1913; March 21, 1913; March 25, 1913. Records of Superior Court, Criminal Division, County of Sacramento, Sacramento City Archives.

39. Ibid., 32.

40. Ibid., 4.

41. Ibid., 37–38.

42. The judge, for one, was convinced that she was congenitally slow, calling her "clouded in her mind" and noting that "she doesn't seem very quick"(35). The defense thought that she was faking her "stupidity" and questioned her on her educational background (44).

43. Case #5196, Transcript of Preliminary Hearing, 60.

44. Ibid., 64.
45. Ibid., 66.
46. Ibid.
47. Ibid., 146.
48. Ibid., 103.
49. Ibid., 113.
50. Ibid., 93.
51. Ibid., 182.
52. Ibid., 173.
53. Ibid., 174.
54. Ibid., 174–175.
55. Ibid., 176.

56. Or other types of "dark" immigrants. See Rosen, *Lost Sisterhood*, chapter 7, for a discussion of the mythology of white slavery.

57. According to the 1900 census, 402 African Americans lived in Sacramento. The town had 1,065 Chinese and 336 Japanese residents (*Twelfth Census of the United States 1900, Volume I*, CXIX). By 1910 there had been little change in the African American and Chinese populations (486 and 1,054, respectively), but the Japanese population had grown to 1,437 (*Thirteenth Census of the United States 1910, Volume II*, p.180).

58. The *Bee* did the same for "Hebrews" and women working for the vote. It seems that only Japanese and Chinese immigrants were excluded from the *Bee*'s liberal constellation. In fact, the McClatchy family was a major participant in the anti-Japanese movement in California. The McClatchys also worked on national immigration restriction.

59. Case #4977, Records of Superior Court, Criminal Division, County of Sacramento, Sacramento City Archives.

60. Case #4977, Transcript of Grand Jury Hearing, 15–25.

61. Ibid., 30. This policeman, Officer Kramer, actually demonstrated a degree of racial tolerance in his impatience with the juror who thought he knew everything. It was Kramer who identified a "respectable" Japanese quarter, an oxymoron for many of the jurors, and it was he who took pains to clarify the misconceptions about the community. Having argued the point about the racial character of the houses and their location, Kramer was asked, "Well, don't all Japanese carry a gun?" One can almost hear the exasperation in his answer, "Sometimes" (35).

62. In fact, Green was the only one of three men arrested between 1911 and 1915 who served time on this charge. A man arrested in 1912 was released, and one arrested in 1913 was convicted but received probation. See General Index, Records of Superior Court, Criminal Division, County of Sacramento, Sacramento City Archives.

63. Case #4920 (*People v. Vernon*), Transcript of Preliminary Hearing, 2. Records of Superior Court, Criminal Division, County of Sacramento, Sacramento City Archives.

64. Case #4919 (*People v. Green*), Transcript of Preliminary Hearing, 12. Records of Superior Court, Criminal Division, County of Sacramento, Sacramento City Archives.

65. Ibid., 5.

66. Goldman, *Gold Diggers and Silver Miners*; Butler, *Daughters of Joy, Sisters of Misery*; and Jacqueline Baker Barnhart, *The Fair But Frail: Prostitution in San Francisco, 1849–1900* (Reno: University of Nevada Press, 1986).

67. Case #4920, Transcript of Preliminary Hearing, 12.

68. Ibid.

Index

Compositor: Impressions Book and Journal Services, Inc.
Text: 11/14 Caledonia
Display: Golden Cockeral Bold
Printer: Edwards Brothers, Inc.
Binder: Edwards Brothers, Inc.